JUMP-START
YOUR
CAREER

TEN TIPS TO GET YOU GOING

CHRIS FONTANELLA

ILLUMIFY
MEDIA.COM

Jump-Start Your Career

The views and opinions expressed in this book are those of the author and do not necessarily reflect the official policy or position of Illumify Media Global.

Published by
Illumify Media Global
www.IllumifyMedia.com
"Let's bring your book to life!"

Library of Congress Control Number:

Paperback ISBN: 978-1-955043-94-6

Typeset by Jen Clark
Cover design by Debbie Lewis

Printed in the United States of America

To my dad, who started at the bottom, made it to the top, and never let it change him.

CONTENTS

INTRODUCTION

GET GOING ON YOUR CAREER

Jack, a recent graduate from Villanova University, recently entered the workforce. After a few weeks on the job, he called his dad and said, "Work is so boring. How do you do this for forty years?" His dad's simple yet inspired response: "One day at a time . . . and you realize work is not life"—an important point of distinction.

Maybe you just graduated from college; maybe you just obtained a two-year associate's degree from a vocational school; or maybe you did neither and decided to enter the workforce straight out of high school. Maybe you know what you want to do career-wise; maybe you do not.

What you do know is that you want the next forty-plus years at work to have purpose. You want what you to do to be meaningful. But you are unfamiliar with the employment terrain you are about to traverse. What can you do to avoid the life of boredom Jack alluded to?

You are at a transition point in your life, one which, to a certain degree, mirrors your departure from adolescence to adulthood. It is time to learn to stand on your own two feet. You may still have the benefit of parental support, or you may not. You may have student loans, or you may not. Regardless, a new chapter in your life is beginning. You are about to take the first steps of your career journey. Your life of employment is about to begin.

You need a job.

And you want your "job" to be more than making money to pay your bills, though that is reason enough to get your ass out of bed each day and log in your eight hours, if not more. But work should be more than just logging time. It should be, as Stephen Pollan and Mark Levine say in their book *Die Broke: A Radical, Four-Part Financial Plan*, "what you do so you can have a life."[1]

For a period of time, my own career lacked rhyme and reason. It did not follow a straight line from point A to point B. My steps were far from calculated. My path: a course blazed by a combination of providence, luck, and intuition, more than anything else. And despite the lack of a "perfect" plan, my career has been rewarding.

But most have no clue how to ensure this is the case: they do not know how to work toward a rewarding career or think a career can even be so. What can you do to inject more meaning into your career, into your forty or so years of employment, so the job is not "boring"?

The following chapters offer ideas on how to posture yourself for a gratifying, noteworthy career. What you will read does not cover the common topics of books of this nature: you will not find tips on résumé writing and interviewing, or steps you should take to ascend the corporate ladder; it does not tell you how to explain the gaps in your résumé, how to negotiate your salary and when to ask for a raise; nor does it tell you how to exit a company without burning a bridge. In sum: it is *not* a how-to manual.

Rather, it offers atypical concepts and ideas intended to shape who you are as a person, which, in turn, should shape your career. Chapter 1 encourages you to find your calling, a word I use interchangeably with career throughout the book.

(The word *calling* means vocation, profession, trade, or occupation, but it can also mean divine summons. Aside from its religious component, a calling is similar to a career in that both relate to what you do for a living and how you spend your time at work.)

Other chapters include topics such as mapping out the career "territory" you want to explore, having ambitious goals for your career, and understanding that achievements depend on the help of others. You will find, in no particular order, a chapter about obstacles, doors that prevent access to your discoveries, and others on letting your work speak for itself and the importance of being willing to start at the bottom. Since careers develop over a span of years, it seemed appropriate to include a section on the benefit of time. Time is an ally, not an enemy, of the career minded. Finally, I discuss the significance of your uniqueness: whatever job you choose to do or calling you seek to fulfill, it must allow *you* to be part of the equation. Any job that asks you to divorce yourself from the work you do is not the job for you.

A couple items of note:

First, the material that follows stems from a story I read about Dr. Kent Weeks, renowned archeologist who discovered the largest subterranean tomb in Egypt, called KV5, which housed the family of Rameses II, Egypt's most accomplished pharaoh. After reading a 1995 *Time* magazine article on Weeks's discovery of KV5, I began to research his life and his life's work; it intrigued me. If looked at through an allegorical lens, the story of Dr. Weeks offers valuable insights to those about to enter the workforce. "Everything's got a moral," says *Alice in Wonderland*'s author Lewis Carroll, "if only you can find it."

Lastly, a feature called Jumper Cables ends each chapter, reviewing key points that can be easily referenced and offering a few exercises that reinforce the material in the chapter. As I note later, why map out a territory of excavation if you have no intention of picking up a shovel to dig? So this section in each chapter includes some simple action steps to charge your engine so you can move toward your goal of a purposeful life of employment.

If you are looking to "jump-start your career" and eager for some tips to do so, please read on.

1 FIND YOUR CALLING

Some struggle to find their calling—not Dr. Kent Weeks. From an early age—eight years old, according to his own recollection—he knew what he wanted to do with his life. Dr. Weeks is Indiana Jones minus movie-making magic, and there is a lot to learn from his career.

After receiving a master's in anthropology from the University of Washington and a doctorate in Egyptology from Yale, he served as professor emeritus of Egyptology and professor of anthropology at the American University in Cairo. Other jobs he held included professorships at the University of Chicago and University of California, Berkeley, an appointment as director of the Theban Mapping Project—for which he is most famous—and assistant curator of Egyptian art at the Metropolitan Museum of Art.

He got lucky when he landed the job at The Met.

At a time when he wondered what next to do with his life —a spot in which you may now find yourself—he bumped into an old colleague and fellow Egyptologist, Henry Fisher. Fisher told him a position had opened at The MET because its associate curator, Erik Young, decided to relocate to New

Zealand to pursue his passion: cabinet making. How fortuitous!

Up to this point, Weeks had had his nose to the grindstone; then a chance moment changed everything. Funny how being diligent often gives birth to opportunity: the harder you work, the luckier you get. And when hard work and luck meet, magic happens.

Magic also happened in 1980 when the Los Angeles Lakers won the championship led by a rookie from Michigan State named Earvin "Magic" Johnson. However, by the end of the following season, the team was in turmoil. They suffered a disgraceful playoff defeat to the Houston Rockets and went from champs to chumps. Off-season trades followed, and management bartered human capital as they saw fit. The Lakers' owners also acquired Mitch Kupchak, a hardworking power forward who could score and rebound, and they struck a deal to keep "Magic" on the payroll. Who wouldn't pony up some shekels for a bit of *magic*?

Still smarting from their play-off loss to the Rockets and angry about the big-dollar contracts awarded to Mitch and Magic, the rest of the team arrived at training camp disgruntled. A tear in the Lakers' garment began to show, and certain players were too happy to tug at it.

Coupled with all this drama, the back office also decided to fire the team's coach, Paul Westhead, even though he had delivered a championship the year prior. (Rumors spread that Magic Johnson had different opinions on offensive strategy, which may have prompted this move.) Owner Jerry Buss thought Pat Riley and Jerry West—former Laker great whose silhouette is on the National Basketball Association logo— would make a great coaching duo. West squashed that idea before it took its first breath and recommended that Riley coach the team on his own. Riley stepped up to the occasion, and West—who seemed bent on pursuing his own calling— eyed another position: general manager.

Looking back on these events, Pat Riley concluded he became the Lakers' head coach "through an accident of history."[1] After eighteen years coming up the ranks—as a player who warmed the bench, as a color commentator next to Chick Hearn, and as the team's "traveling secretary" and assistant coach—he finally got his shot. He was in the right place at the right time, and unexpected events worked in his favor: a bit of luck tied everything together.

Before running for the office of president, Barack Obama consulted Ted Kennedy, a senior Democrat who knew everything about politics and the White House. Obama, who was busy with community meetings and projects in Chicago, hoped Kennedy would opine on when would be the right time for him to run. To spur on the young senator, Kennedy offered the following apt adage: "You don't choose the time. The time chooses you."[2] Indeed it does. Following an arduous campaign trail, Barack Obama's tenure as the forty-fourth president of the United States began on January 20, 2009. He noticed and took advantage of a changing political landscape and seized his destiny.

After almost thirty years of finding jobs for people, I am still amazed at how opportunities materialize: some stem from an employee who quits to start another job elsewhere; others crop up because people get fired; sometimes management, concerned mainly with the organization's interests and with no regard for others, makes decisions that impact staff; and still others seem to materialize out of thin air. At times, the circumstances that create these open roles appear massaged—some might say manipulated—by an invisible hand. That appears to be the case with Riley and Obama, and with Dr. Weeks, who landed a gig because Erik Young quit to pursue a different career—one man's love for crafting wood made room for another man's love of digging in the dirt.

In an interview, Dr. Weeks described his scenario as "absolutely, accidentally perfect."[3] In other words, he got lucky—an unplanned plan came together. He found himself in the right place at the right time. He then seized the occasion and went on to a celebrated career.

How or why this happens is hard to say. When it happens, though, it is remarkable.

Something similar happened in my career. For personal reasons, I had laid aside my aspiration to be a minister and took a job at a bank. (There was nothing magical about it. My dad knew someone there who offered me a job.) After a couple of years there, a Minnesota-based bank purchased the division in which I worked. No one saw that coming, except, of course, the powers that be who orchestrated the deal.

At the time, I lived in California and opted not to relocate and then found employment in the staffing industry, which prompted amazing career experiences: participating in an initial public offering, starting a business and selling it, and founding a second company—none of which would have happened had Bank of America not decided to divest itself of its corporate trust division. That decision shaped my career, even though I was unaware of the management discussions that took place behind the scenes.

Sometimes moments of destiny spring from unexpected events; within them may lie your calling, that which helps define who you are and what you choose to do.

Later in his career, another unexpected event presented itself to Dr. Weeks. While he served as professor of Egyptology at the American University of Cairo, Egyptian authorities considered a proposal to erect a parking lot near the location where King Tutankhamun's tomb had been discovered—a significant area to archeologists like Weeks. Of all places, why here? Why build a parking structure in the area where a notable discovery had already been made? Weeks must have thought to himself, *Upon further exploration, more may be found.*

Not comfortable trampling another man's grave or even

getting close to one, he petitioned to do one final dig to ensure nothing of importance had been missed by his archeological predecessors. Even though others had lost interest in this parcel of land, Weeks believed it still held importance.

Egyptologists know the history of this site. In 1820 James Burton explored the plot, and one hundred years later, Howard Carter invested considerable time on it. Both concluded no major discoveries were left to be found, and thus, the zone around King Tut's tomb lacked significance. Those recommending the parking lot concurred; Weeks did not.

There is more than what meets the eye—the activity taking place above the surface did not prevent him from seeing worlds below the surface.

Good thing Weeks ignored the opinions of his predecessors: he ultimately discovered the largest subterranean tomb located in the Valley of the Kings, which housed the sons of Ramesses II, referred to by present-day Egyptians as Ramesses the Greatest. (A name well-deserved based on his notable achievements, which included building more temples, obelisks, and monuments than any other pharaoh. He also procreated like a cottontail rabbit. He is said to have fathered over one hundred children.)

Some speculate Ramesses II was Moses' nemesis noted in the book of Exodus and immortalized on film by Yul Brynner in *The Ten Commandments*. According to Scripture, and the film, God dealt Egypt a final death blow in the form of a plague that killed the firstborn of all Egyptians, including Pharaoh's son. The graveyard identified by Weeks may be that of this son and his family, though Weeks is quick to point out his discovery is not intended to prove or disprove biblical references.

The story about Dr. Weeks and his noteworthy discovery reminds us of a couple of basic career truths: opportunities of destiny present themselves as you are busy at work, and that which is worth finding is worth working to find. Weeks worked hard to make his dream a reality, but he also got lucky. The opportunity means nothing if you do nothing with it.

Imagine the countless shovelfuls of dirt and debris Dr. Weeks and his team hauled away; imagine the dust; imagine how he and his team had to crawl through the dimly lit shaft; and imagine a door at the end of this claustrophobic underground journey. That door blocked access to the greatest discovery in the history of Egyptology. To pry it open was no easy task. Beyond it, a statue of Osiris, Egyptian god of the afterlife, stood as sentinel over an impressive labyrinth of corridors and doors fanning out on all sides. After years of wearisome work, Weeks and his team discovered the resting place of Ramesses II's royal sons and their children—an enormous mausoleum compared to others found over the years.

In the course of doing what he felt called to do, he made the discovery of a lifetime. And if not for Dr. Weeks, this part of Egypt's past would have remained hidden, buried under years of accumulating sand.

You are called to do something with your life, and you are about to start your career. You need to identify the overarching theme that provides the reasons you get up and go to work each day—your reason for being. Maybe you only have a general idea of what you want to do. Maybe you know exactly what field you want to enter. Regardless, there are discoveries that lie in wait and are for you alone to find.

What remains hidden if you do not find and pursue your calling? What will others fail to see if you do not do what you were meant to do?

Your calling, your career, has more far-reaching ramifications than you can imagine.

Jumper Cables

- The word *calling* means vocation, profession, trade, or occupation, but it can also mean a divine summons, as if it has a sense of destiny associated with it. Aside from its religious connotation, a *calling* is similar to a *career* in that both relate to what you do for a living and how you spend your time at work.
- Learning your calling can happen a number of ways, including through "accidents of history." No one can tell you what your calling is. You must learn that on your own.
- Remember: oftentimes, moments of destiny spring from unexpected events. Keep an ear to the ground to listen for activity that may be taking place below the surface.
- Take a moment to write down any interesting developments or unplanned events that have happened in your life. How have they influenced the direction of your journey thus far?
- List five things you love to do and identify careers that align with those interests.
- Opportunities mean nothing if you do nothing with them.
- Good fortune comes to the industrious. Work your ass off, and when luck knocks, let it in.

2 MAP OUT YOUR AREA OF EXPLORATION

You may be wondering, "How do I find my calling?" and "How do I determine what to do career-wise?" Or asked another way, "Who do I want to be, and what do I want to do for a living?" Good questions. My response might not be one you like.

Those questions cannot be answered by me or anyone else: you must answer them for yourself.

For some, the realization happens with fanfare, like it did for Paul the Apostle: "As he neared Damascus on his journey, suddenly a light from heaven flashed around him" (Acts 9:3). Who wouldn't know the plan for their life after that? For Ishmael in Melville's *Moby Dick*, it was "an everlasting itch for things remote" that made him sail the open seas; he fulfilled his mission in life on the whaleship *Pequod*. Ernest Gallo, famous vintner, said his aunt, who claimed she could tell fortunes, predicted he would be successful in business, either in oil or in wine. It happened to be wine.

For others, like actress Jean Smart—known for her breakout role in *Designing Women* and more recently her work in *Fargo*, *Mare of Easttown*, and *Hacks*—a sense of being drawn to the stage gripped her during her senior year in high school.

For others still, including myself, an unexpected event may lead to it, like a corporate transaction that relocates your job to Minnesota, and there ain't no way in hell you are moving there. As mentioned, Pat Riley fits this category. Many were surprised when Paul Westhead got fired, but it opened the door for Riley.

And then there are those like Dr. Weeks—and my daughter, who has always had a *thing* for music—who know from an early age the direction their career and life will take. Early accounts of legendary baseball player Derek Jeter say he was forever carrying around his baseball glove, always on the lookout for a game. And family members recall how, from an early age, he talked about baseball all the time. Pete Townshend, guitarist and song writer for The Who, said his infancy was "steeped in awareness of the mystery and romance" of the music his father played.[1] Somehow that must have rubbed off on him.

Callings are not mass-produced. There are no cookie-cutter careers, vocations without distinction: each is tailor-made. And finding yours can happen in any number of ways, so unfortunately, no specific steps can be offered on how to find it. But I can tell you this: for most, finding it requires digging. And if you must dig, you should first make a map.

Dr. Weeks understood the importance of cartography, the practice of making and using maps. In fact, he is famous for his Theban Mapping Project, an archeological expedition devoted to ancient Egypt, with a goal to create a map of the Valley of the Kings. Successful archeology depends on map making—as do successful careers—for maps detail, as best as possible, the ground excavated.

If your job requires you to draw or make blueprint designs, as it does for an interior designer or architectural engineer, this may be all in a day's work and nothing could be easier: mine does not. As a result, my map designs look unrefined, lacking sophistication and style, like a kindergartner's crayon scribbles. But as bad as they are, my doodles still point me in a direction.

And that is what matters.

Initial sketch work for career maps includes lines represented by experiences, education, interests, dreams, desires, talents, and more: a bachelor of science in accounting or computer engineering, an interest in marine biology or the arts, a talent for working with your hands, a curiosity about world religions, a challenging childhood that drives you to succeed, a love of children, being a single parent, a passion for sports or a desire to perform—or none of these, but others. Whatever these lines may be, mark them down: they make up the contours of your map that offer a general direction to your excavation site, where your discovery waits to be found.

Time spent making a map sets the stage for your discovery.

Over time, however, you will need to amend your map: first sketches are rarely final sketches. Even skilled archeologists, like Dr. Weeks, revise their maps often, and the best map makers use an eraser as much if not more than the pencil itself. Like crossword puzzles, maps should never be done in pen; corrections will need to be made—a fact many choose *not* to accept. Map makers, like authors, understand the importance of editing.

Practically speaking, this means you should not rigidly define your map's boundary lines. Some people think the bolder the lines, the better—and more accurate—the map. But nothing is further from the truth; such map-drawing boldness is presumptive and does not account for the winds of change that life may blow your way. As you begin to map out your career and establish the border lines of your calling, you may be tempted to make such bold marks.

Stark and vivid map lines—on paper and in your mind— are hard to erase, and you will find, as I have, that change— whether it originates from choices you made or otherwise— also plays a role in map creation.

Consider this: your career, as has been briefly alluded to above, consists of a variety of components—education, interests, life and work experiences—making it more complex than you think. *Webster's New Universal Unabridged Dictionary* defines *complex* in a nuanced fashion, noting its Latin derivation from a word that means "to weave and to braid." Complex constructs consist of interlaced *strands* that form a more intricate pattern, like a stylish hair braid or boat rope.

Your career will be made of different "strands" woven together, or, in keeping with the map metaphor, lines that are drawn or spliced together. Frankenstein-like, most careers are stitched together with various parts to form something greater —and stronger—than each part can be separately. Maps are made not of one line but many, and multiple pieces comprise a career: they are a cluster of distinctive characteristics.

The sketch work of my original map may help you understand what I mean. It outlined—in striking fashion, I might add—a life of service to God, a minister's life: years studying theology; learning to read and write biblical Greek; serving as youth minister and worship leader; leading Bible studies; and pastoring a church—actions analogous to digging on an excavation site. Yet, after all this, I did a stint in banking and then became a business development professional in the staffing industry, finding jobs for accounting and finance professionals. Go figure!

How does someone with a master of arts in theological studies end up finding jobs for certified public accountants? He does so if he amends his map.

Later in my career, I resigned from a company after five years—another decision that triggered major map amendments and interesting career developments. My time with that firm deepened my knowledge of the staffing industry and broadened my sales experience, but after the company's initial public offering (IPO), the organization changed. Fearing individuality and uncomfortable with staff taking their own approach to sales, its management sought to homogenize people and processes—uniformity usurped diversity.

Knowing I would not thrive in such an environment, I sought greener pastures elsewhere. When a more attractive opportunity presented itself—one offering better pay, a better bonus plan, and a better situation in general—I explored it. But the grass is not always greener on the other side of the hill; that job lasted three months.

As I pondered my next move, an unexpected phone call from a former coworker led to a discussion about starting a firm of our own, which we did. After a period of success, a national consulting firm purchased our company. Many years later, that consulting firm was purchased by the company my partner and I had originally worked for before we ventured out on our own. And it turned out management there was still upset with me for leaving. As a result, they decided to exclude me from the acquisition. Left out of the deal, I started another business—this time on my own.

All this to say, I have edited and reconfigured my map many times. Circumstances change. When they do, you must adapt—and not overthink what prompted the change. Time is better spent editing your map, rather than agonizing and mulling over why the landscape has changed.

To help with map design and redesign, archeologists use theodolites—surveying instruments with a rotating telescope for measuring horizontal and vertical angles—to analyze and re-analyze landscapes. It allows them to see new angles and dimensions that escaped prior observation. For the career-minded—but especially new entrants into the workforce—change is one instrument that affords you an opportunity to analyze and re-analyze employment topography.

As my career scenery changed, it prompted questions: Was an invisible hand manipulating events? Were unexpected occurrences leading me—pushing me—toward a moment of destiny? Does being cut out *of* a deal mean you're cut out *for* another? Were these new developments "accidents of history"?

The point of all this: no matter how detailed and defined the lines of your map, no matter how refined your sketch, no matter how in-depth your draft, you cannot account for everything. Adjustments must be made along the way, and transition points in your career—some might call them crossroads —invite reliance on intuition, a more uncommon instrument with which to survey your career.

When the map lines you have sketched no longer match your real-life experience; when, for some strange reason, you feel compelled to pursue a calling that does not correspond to your declared major; when, out of nowhere, the company you work for downsizes employees and you get the axe; when your entrepreneurial venture encounters a setback; or maybe when you reach a *door* that stands between you and a discovery—let your instincts direct you.

Call it a sixth sense. Call it divination. Call it clairvoyance. Call it whatever you want and define it however you want, but just know there will be times you should toss the map out the window and make sense of things without having all the answers. Sometimes you just have to "go with your gut."

As a kid, Russian-born Igor Sikorsky heard numerous lectures from his father on electricity, astronomy, and physics, which fostered within him an inquisitiveness about those subjects. No wonder then, from an early age, he dreamed of flying machines. He studied engineering in Russia's Naval Academy, and before he turned twenty years old, his fantasies about aeronautics became reality: he constructed a helicopter.

Soon after, he designed airplanes for Russia, including bombers used in World War I. Later, he emigrated to the United States but failed to find work with a U.S. aeronautics company. Instead, he chose to teach about it. Restless with that "career," he decided to start his own company, the Sikorsky Aero Engineering Corporation.

In a written piece called *A Mysterious Faculty*, Sikorsky bats around the idea of intuition—what some might call thinking outside the box—and its relation to success. After admitting that the true nature of intuition cannot be understood, he concludes it is "an extremely primitive and barely noticeable . . . faculty of higher order."[2] Thomas Edison and Henry Ford succeeded, he says, because their intuition allowed them to *envision* the future and then "direct their efforts accordingly."[3] Edison admitted as much, saying he received *impressions* from the universe that had to be worked out.

Change forces you to consider new dimensions, and often-times intuition is what helps you size up those changes so you can amend your map and better direct your efforts.

Before you dig, then, take time to map out your area of exploration. During excavation, you may uncover something that changes everything. When that happens, reassess and redefine your map: adjustments may need to be made to account for feelings within and factors without that have altered the terrain. And do not ignore your intuition: it may offer insights needed to guide you into your future.

Jumper Cables

- Take time to map out your career. Get paper and pencil (for this exercise you can use pen), and notate your interests, dreams and desires, your college major or emphasis in vocational school, hobbies, likes and dislikes, and anything that tugs at your heart or fills your mind.
- What you have listed represents lines on your map. Determine what careers relate to them and head in that direction. And let the excavation begin.
- Remember: maps are meant to be tweaked. Do not be surprised if you need to make amendments. You

are in good company: everyone, at one time or another, redesigns their map. Never be disheartened by the map-editing process—those changes possess destiny-shaping power.

- Every now and then, take a fresh look at your map and compare it to your current life of employment. Note where the lines of your map match up and where they do not. Make adaptations when and where necessary.

- Intuition may be a more "primitive" way to make sense of things, but it offers "out of the box" thoughts on how to redefine your career and redirect your efforts to make your future a reality.

3 BE AMBITIOUS

In an article entitled "Living in the Past – Egyptologist Kent R. Weeks, Old Lyme," which covers the span of Dr. Weeks's life's work and purpose, Rona Mann describes the Thebban Mapping Project as "an *ambitious effort* to photograph and map every temple and tomb in the Theban Necropolis" (italics mine).[1] No wonder his grand goal garnered worldwide attention and stimulated renewed interest in Egyptology.

When you sketch your career map, make it an exceedingly *ambitious effort*. In other words, *dream big*.

As cliché as this phrase and others like it may be—*the sky is the limit, anything is possible*, and *the world is your oyster*—overuse does not diminish their meaningfulness; it validates their importance. The example set by Dr. Weeks says starting small is never wrong; thinking small is, always. So, waste no time conceiving pocket-sized plans. Instead, dream up grand goals.

The beginning of any venture, and especially the start of your career, is the perfect time to set your sights high. To achieve anything worthwhile, you should attempt even those things that seem impossible. Now is the best time in your career to forsake insignificant objectives, inferior goals, and unimaginative designs: exceptional enterprises seldom spring from dainty dreams.

In the 1830s, a crop of talented, hopeful, and aspiring Americans with outsized dreams in their hearts set out for Paris, at that time a city more advanced in medicine, engineering, music, art, theater, and other aspects of life. People like Oliver Wendell Holmes (physician and poet, notable for his medical research and teaching), James Fenimore Cooper (author of *The Last of the Mohicans*), Charles Sumner (U.S. Senator, who would lead anti-slavery campaigns), Samuel F.B. Morse (painter, more well-known for his single-wire telegraph system known as Morse code), Emma Willard (founder of a female seminary and fierce advocate of higher education for women), and Augustus Saint-Gaudens (sculptor who became famous for his monuments of the American Civil War), all went to Paris to pursue "the call" that pulsed in their hearts. "They spoke of [Paris] then as the dream of a lifetime, and for many, for all the difficulties and setbacks," says David McCullough in *The Greater Journey: Americans in Paris,* "it was to be one of the best times ever."[2]

Whether you know it or not, starting your career offers you the same chance: an opportunity at "the dream of a lifetime . . . one of the best times ever."

None of these dream-filled Americans knew what life outside their country was like or how different it would be—similar to feelings you may be experiencing now as you step outside the life of college or vocational school and commence another within an unfamiliar work world. Most had never been to sea or even boarded a seagoing vessel. And despite having apprehensions, their ambition remained undaunted by the threats—real or imagined—that crossing the sea might have presented.

Their lives underwent a sea change as they faced the dangers of the sea. Similarly, as you board your boat of employment and begin to traverse unknown waters, you, too, will experience the damp and drizzly days at sea and its dark and dangerous nights. But as Melville reminds us in *Moby Dick*, "Better is it to perish in that howling infinite, than be ingloriously dashed upon the lee." In other words, to face treacherous waters in pursuit of your dream is superior to the security offered by the shore.

Scientists believe just about everyone dreams each time they sleep. But how do big dreams fill your heart while you lie awake, thinking about what next to do with your life? How do you catch a monumental vision for your career? How do you come up with an exceedingly ambitious plan?

You may find my answer to these questions irksome because, as is the case with identifying your calling, each individual comes to those answers on their own, in their own way, and in their own time. That said, there is something that can help: mysticism. At every stage, but especially the beginning stage of devising an exceedingly ambitious plan, mysticism better postures you to catch dreams: mystical thinking fosters an environment whereby big dreams enter hearts.

More than likely, you are now envisioning monks, nuns, and others dedicated to a life of contemplation, and wondering if it might be best to skip this chapter. You may be asking, "How in the world does this relate to my career?" It does; stay with me.

The strict definition of mysticism may be why you have the heebie-jeebies about my suggestion: it is, according to Lexico.com, the "belief that union with or absorption into the Deity or the absolute . . . may be attained through contemplation and self-surrender."

Quite religious sounding, I know. It does conjure up images of those who chant, rub prayer beads, or kneel on prayer mats, and of those who opt for a cloistered life. Indeed, many religious persons adhere to mystical practices like these and more. Famous mystics like Meister Eckhart, Teresa of

Avila, and St. John of the Cross—a few of the more famous ones—tapped into a range of mystical exercises to connect with God.

The goal of a mystic is a *spiritual connection* with a higher power. They look beyond the physical world and attempt to "see" and "hear" what cannot be seen or heard with natural eyes and ears. For them, a nonmaterial invisible realm exists, something akin to the spirit world of the American Indian.

Yet, after researching the etymology of the word, I propose that a simpler definition—one stripped of religious coloring—exists: the act of being contemplative, meditative, or reflective. The Greek word from which mysticism stems, *muein*, means to close one's eyes or lips. In other words, it is challenging to *connect*—with a higher power, yourself, or anyone, for that matter—if you are visually distracted or busy blabbing. The basic formula for mysticism, then, looks like this: close your eyes, shut your mouth, and open your ears.

Back in the day, elementary school kids needed a hall pass to go to the restroom. If you roamed the halls without one, an adult—typically someone who looked like a warden at Shawshank State Prison—would escort you to the principal's office. Mysticism, in the sense in which I have defined it, is a "hall pass" that grants your mind the freedom to wander; your thoughts have permission to roam other "dimensions"—and dream big.

Some believe contemplation, meditation, and reflection should be reserved for religious environments only: churches, synagogues, mosques, other houses of worship, or even the sanctuary of nature. Mysticism, according to them, should not be practiced anywhere and everywhere. Hogwash!

You can contemplate anywhere: sitting in your kitchen while your mind sits elsewhere; resting in bed as your mind turns over a particular idea; or while driving a car and your thoughts stew about other matters. You are physically present somewhere but lost in thought.

For me, music tends to foster an environment in which my mind feels free to wander. Without fail, my mind roams every time I hear the Christmas hymn "O Night Divine," especially when sung by an accomplished choir.

O night divine! The stars are brightly shining.
   It is the night of the dear Savior's birth:
   O hearts that weep, in lonely sorrow pining.
   Behold, he comes with redeeming love to earth!
   The light of hope now the waking world rejoices.
   For brightly breaking, there dawns a glorious morn.
   Fall on your knees.
   O hear the angel voices!
   O night divine.

As its chorus echoes in my head, I "hear" angels' voices, and I "see" the glow of redeeming light. Majestic tones carry me to heavenly heights and then escort me back to Earth, where, in my mind, I fall on my knees. When I finally snap out of this mystical moment, I realize the song transported me to a nonphysical realm and back—all while seated in a pew.

The same thing happened when I attended Grateful Dead concerts, where the band would go off on their infamous improvisational jam sessions, taking Deadheads on a "magical musical tour" to celestial places. The band's unique musicality—psychedelic rock fused with folk, jazz, blues, bluegrass, and country—took me on a "trip" without leaving the auditorium. The music carried me to places beyond the arena.

Even classical music affects me this way. The music of French composer Claude Debussy, which they say is based on poetry, a writing style written by introspective souls which fosters reflection and contemplation, takes me places. Quiet symphonies of sound, his compositions "shuttle" me to an otherworldly country of the mind.

Here on Earth, a car transports me from one place to another, no easy task in Southern California, as those of us who traverse the spacious city of Los Angeles know. No LA resident can avoid its streets. Whether cruising in style or piloting a clunker, drive you must. No one walks in Los Angeles, as the Missing Persons song says. Its freeways—the 5, 10, 57, 60, 101, 110, 210, 405—are congested with maniacal motorists in metallic machines, making their way down concrete rivers. "Rush hour" is anything but smooth sailing.

Being a salesman, I have traveled these roads often. My job requires me to visit clients at their places of work, or at restaurants close by if wining and dining figures into the sales equation. Regardless, for years I have bobbed and weaved around cars, letting the California freeways, with their never-ending traffic jams and slow crawls, get the best of me. Until . . .

Until I mentally transformed my vehicle into a *sanctuary* for mysticism. Now, car time—no matter how congested the roads may be—offers opportunities for meditative reflection and dreaming big, as my heart and mind roam the halls of what is possible.

Recognizing a common theme among myths of different countries and peoples, mythologists discuss the importance of mysticism and suggest isolating yourself in a walled garden—a place of quiet retreat to restore your soul, to be introspective, and to allow your mind to wander. In the garden, says Robert Bly in his *New York Times* bestseller *Iron John: A Book about Men*, "a [person] finds the wealth of the psyche."[3]

And hears messages . . .

After thirty years of working in corporate America and placing people in jobs within it, I concluded no better way exists to posture yourself to hear a *message*—an exceedingly ambitious plan perhaps—than making time for moments of reflection. In my experience, that is when life-changing, meaningful messages—big-dream ideas—seem to emerge.

They surprise us like storms that come with no warning. Theories about how they spring up and why this happens make for interesting dialogue at dinner parties, but in truth, no one can wrap their arms around such ethereal mysteries. For the sake of argument, let us just say it happens because "transmissions" are trying to "break through" to the intended recipients. When we adopt a contemplative posture, we prepare a path for messages to penetrate the noise that normally enshrouds us.

Mysticism matters because it increases the potential for big dreams to reach your heart and mind.

But a big dream does not become reality on its own. You must act upon that dream. Big dreams become reality by taking little steps.

Case in point: Dave Phinney. Best known for his wines Orin Swift and The Prisoner, he achieved success by disrupting a profession known for its zealots of tradition. The old guard preferred not to mess with the formula for making great wine. But Phinney wanted to make great wines available at an affordable price, as well as remove industry snobbery—and he wanted to accomplish both by crafting a "blend." He also adopted an atypical artistic approach to his wine labels. He believed a catchy label had the power to draw in a buyer, but the flavor of the wine would keep folks coming back for more. The wine industry now knows the name Dave Phinney.

But Phinney was not an overnight success. Here are some steps that turned his dream into a reality and got him to where he is today:

- He grew up in Los Angeles, attended the University of Arizona, and majored in political science.
- He worked as a public defender and a U.S.

23

congressional leader and ditched both jobs to work in a wine shop. (Ditching one career for another is a common link among career heroes.)

- With the help of an agriculture professor from the University of Arizona, he planted Zinfandel and Petite Sirah vines and got some hands-on experience. But deep down, he really wanted to work a harvest in Napa Valley.
- He submitted dozens of résumés to well-known wine producers and eventually landed a job with Robert Mondavi Winery.
- Later he studied winemaking under Dean Sylvester at Whitehall Lane Winery. Around that time he met his future wife, who happened to be the daughter of winery founder Tom Leonardini. (A fortuitous meeting, to say the least. Luck always visits the industrious.)
- He decided to make his own wine.
- He produced wine blending whatever grapes he could get his hands on.
- He made 385 cases of The Prisoner, which debuted at twenty-five dollars per bottle in the year 2000.
- Within a few years, Phinney produced eighty thousand cases. (That's growth worth raising a glass to.)
- Ernst and Julio Gallo acquired Orin Swift Cellars and Locations, another of Phinney's brands, for an undisclosed amount.

Phinney—poli-sci candidate, public defender, U.S. congressional leader turned vintner—mapped out his big dreams and took small steps to bring them to fruition. His approach, like that of Dr. Weeks, reminds us that success rarely happens overnight, though we may think it does because the spotlight on those who have "arrived" seems brightest. The reality: most *arrive* after many small steps—like the decision to board a boat crossing the Atlantic—without which, the big dreams in your heart and mind never happen.

As you prepare to embark on your career journey, carve out some time for contemplation. "Steal away" to a quiet place. ("Steal Away" is a black American or Negro spiritual term with a double meaning: "steal away" to Jesus, on the surface, meant dying and going to heaven, but it also symbolized escaping to freedom. It is used here metaphorically to represent finding freedom in your mind.) Take some time off from your TV and ignore your smartphone for an hour. Close your eyes and sit in silence. Then, listen. Escape to a place of freedom, and partake in moments of quiet solitude that promote an environment where you can dream big.

To be clear, I am not advocating for or recommending a cloistered, monastic life, although one should feel free to walk that road if compelled to do so. Godspeed to you. Neither am I trying to *convert* you in any way, like some annoying TV preacher who feasts on your wallet but starves your soul. My preaching days have been over for some time, and it has been even longer since I performed drama on the streets of Amsterdam to proselytize and "win souls" for the kingdom of heaven. My motives are less zealous: I am only trying to *convince* you that mysticism matters because it fosters an atmosphere in which big dreams live. But remember: big dreams also require taking small steps toward their realization.

Jumper Cables

- The start of your career is the best time to forsake inconsequential objectives, abandon inferior goals, and cast aside unimaginative designs.
- What does an exceedingly ambitious plan for your career look like? List five wild and crazy ideas on a

note card. Tape it somewhere where you can see it every day.

- Remember: dainty dreams seldom lead to exceptional enterprises. To start small is fine, but to think small is not.
- Mysticism is a belief that you can connect with the Deity through contemplation and self-surrender. A simpler definition is this: an act of being contemplative, meditative, and reflective. The word's Greek origin suggests closing your eyes and mouth and listening.
- Take fifteen minutes each day to reflect and contemplate and listen for "messages." Jot down in a notebook any thoughts that come to you. Create a road map based on those messages.
- Little steps lead to the fulfillment of big dreams. Make two columns on a piece of paper, and on one side write down the steps you have already taken and on the other, those you have not. What do you need to do to move what is listed in the "steps not taken" column into the "steps taken" column?

4 SEE UNSEEN WORLDS

In a 1988 *National Geographic* article entitled "Exploring Cradle Earth," its author stated something along these lines: Aside from the discoveries themselves, maps for others to follow are the most important legacy left by explorers. If true, what else can those commencing their careers learn from the map work of Dr. Weeks? One lesson might be this: your discovery may be beyond your vision but never beyond your reach—what you see above ground does not disprove the actuality of what lies below ground.

Dr. Weeks understood the importance of cartography, the study and practice of making and using maps. His map outlined a comprehensive architectural plan of the Valley of the Kings, the chosen burial place for most of Egypt's New Kingdom rulers. Its images show split-level designs, ascending and descending stairways, and corridors sprawling out on all sides—it depicts an underground world, like the vast system of tunnels underneath Disney World's Magic Kingdom. (The technical term for these types of tunnels is utilidors, short for utility corridors, underground passages that allow Disney employees to provide park support, like trash removal, without ruining the illusion of a magical environment the park seeks to create for its visitors.)

Tourists at KV5, as the subterranean tomb came to be called, are under no illusion as to what they are seeing. Thanks to Dr. Weeks, the world can now see it with their own eyes. But absent his belief that an unseen ancient civilization resided below the surface, the largest subterranean tomb in the Valley of the Kings would never have been found. Simply put: no belief, no digging; no digging, no discovery. Why dig if you are convinced nothing lies below the surface?

His work on KV5 argues against superficiality, rigid unwillingness to penetrate the surface. His life's work tells you one-dimensional perspectives are insufficient: buried treasure cannot be found by surface-level undertakings.

In *The Twilight Zone*, Rod Serling, screenwriter, producer, and narrator, ponders the potential reality of unseen worlds, what he called "dimensions of imagination." The show asks viewers to consider a peculiar possibility: the existence of other realms, ones "as vast as space and as timeless as infinity." Its introduction—narrated by Serling in an unmistakable measured voice—bids us to walk through doors that lead to "a dimension not only of sight and sound but of mind."

Those dimensions, we are told, open with a "key of imagination." In his book, *The Doors of Perception*, Aldous Huxley—an English writer with an interest in philosophical mysticism and multidimensional outlooks—prescribes ingesting peyote to open those doors, a suggestion many Grateful Dead concert attendees appreciated. We need not go to such lengths to experience other dimensions. Still, Huxley makes an interesting point: a less superficial and imaginative point of view can help you *see* more than what meets the eye. Peyote is not necessarily needed, but a figurative shovel is.

Over the years, many shovel-carrying imaginative professionals—visionaries often criticized by their contemporaries for their ability to *see* what others could not—have approached their careers this way.

Here are a few:

- Andrew Carnegie, visionary and map manipulator, left Pennsylvania Railroad and struck out on his own to start Keystone Bridge Works. Eventually he founded Carnegie Steel, which, at the time, accounted for 25 percent of the steel sold in the United States. He recognized the change in the landscape of America and propelled the expansion of the American steel industry and then became a leading philanthropist in the United States and the British Empire.
- The imaginative J. C. Penney resketched his map throughout his career. His redrafts started after he purchased one-third of a dry goods company from his employer. Then, under the name Golden Rule Store—a name conveying his values around doing unto others what you would have done to you—he opened thirteen stores of his own. Later, he expanded and operated 175 stores. (It's a different story today for JCPenney the company. They almost went bankrupt in 2020 because management ignored changing market conditions, which was a perfect time to redesign their corporate map.)
- On September 16, 1985, Steve Jobs—arguably one of the most visionary figures in corporate history—was forced out of Apple, the company he founded. Different factors contributed to this: a woefully slow computer, problems with its internal hard disk drive, declining sales, and the loss of a boardroom battle with then CEO John Sculley, whom Jobs hired. Jobs never sketched this event

on his original map, but it prompted him to reimagine his career: he started a new company called NsXT, which he later sold to Apple for $400 million. Not long after, Jobs became Apple's CEO. How is that for "absolutely, accidentally perfect"?

It dawned on me as I lay awake one morning in bed that what I am suggesting is equally as odd as Huxley's prescription. In essence, what I am suggesting is this: believe in the unseen. Or, stated another way: have faith.

Carnegie possessed it when he walked away from Pennsylvania Railroad and began to revolutionize the steel industry in America. J. C. Penney possessed it when he redefined the boundaries of his map and decided to own his own stores. Steve Jobs possessed it too. Even after being fired from the company he founded, he envisioned another company, which he later sold to Apple, and after all was said and done, he became Apple's CEO. And Dr. Weeks possessed it when he petitioned Egyptian authorities for time to further explore the site near King Tut's tomb, a request that allowed him to turn over more ground in the hope of finding an unseen world.

Each saw what others could not see—and then shoveled away until the invisible became visible.

In a technological world where everything magically appears before our eyes with a tap on a keyboard, no one seems interested anymore in monotonous menial tasks, like digging—moving earth one shovelful at a time gets old really quick. Digging takes forever compared to a click on a computer mouse or a tap on a keypad, and hauling away detritus loses its luster fast.

In his book *The Ride of a Lifetime*, Robert Iger, former CEO of the Walt Disney Company, tells readers that as a kid one of his jobs was "cleaning gum from the bottom of a thousand desks."[1] While he recognized the character-building nature of this exercise, he also said it created a "tolerance for monotony."[2] In other words, monotonous tasks—as humdrum and time-consuming as they may be—are worth tolerating if they yield something of value. Monotony can be tolerated if one's efforts are rewarded: mundane tasks hold more importance than you realize.

Discoveries are the best antidote for drudgery.

And that is why archeologists persist in their excavation efforts. They maintain hope of finding something—anything. Tedious toil and tiresome tasks are endured because they know —even though they cannot always see what they seek—that "relics" of value lie sleeping in subterranean sites and that their persistence will pay off.

Nothing requires persistence like archeology. It is the ongoing and continual study of human history and prehistory through the excavation of sites. Even after an archeologist finds an artifact from some bygone world, he or she will continue to dig further and burrow deeper into the terrain: an initial discovery is tempered by a level of discontentment and dissatisfaction—in their minds, finding one item means other finds are a shovelful away.

Archeologists never dig just to dig; they dig in hope of a discovery.

Most treasures lie underground, buried in dark places, hidden from the expansive reach of the sun. Superficial archeologists never find them. They are found, rather, by those who look beyond and dig below the surface, by those determined to scrape past the outer layer.

Your willingness to dig—monotonously shovel until a discovery is made—has a direct relationship to your ability to "see" what cannot be seen: you will pick up a shovel if you believe buried treasure exists. If you don't, you won't. The hardworking archeologist knows casual glances, quick inspections, and slaphappy surveys of the surface—shallow attempts at discovery—yield limited rewards.

If you hope to establish a career of significance, you must

function as an ardent "archeologist" who believes in unseen worlds. Once you catch a vision of the invisible world you seek to find, grab your map and shovel, bring your Finds Brushes, trowel, theodolite, adze, and dustpan, and head to your territory of exploration. Then, dig! Only a fool sits idly at an excavation, hoping archeological finds of great worth will resurrect themselves from their chambers of rest. Such luck rarely, if ever, knocks on the doors of those without dirt under their fingernails.

Jumper Cables

- Maps guide you to a location. Career maps guide you to a field you want to explore. Your willingness to excavate that territory has a direct correlation to your belief that a discovery can be made.
- A discovery may be beyond your vision but is not beyond your reach. It may be unseen, but that does not mean it does not exist.
- One must have faith—belief in what cannot be seen—to dig. Otherwise, why dig?
- Many imaginative, visionary professionals—like Andrew Carnegie, J. C. Penney, and Steve Jobs—started their careers believing in what others could not see. Who else can you think of that was mocked for their "visions"? Research their career.
- List five things you believe exist that cannot be seen.
- Remember: digging can be pure monotony, but a discovery offsets drudgery.
- The Scriptures say, "Seek and you shall find." I say, "Dig and you shall discover."

5 ACHIEVEMENTS: THE WHOLE TRUTH, NOTHING BUT THE TRUTH

YOU HAVE A VISION FOR YOUR CAREER, YOU HAVE MAPPED out territory to explore, a discovery awaits, and you understand the necessity of shoveling. What more do you need to know, or what should you keep in mind?

As I dug around Dr. Weeks's story, I found this artifact, an important career truth to remember: achievements seldom happen without help.

As you launch your career, imbed this unalterable maxim in your heart and mind: achievements are not solo efforts. The story of Dr. Weeks's KV5 discovery conveys his unashamed reliance on others, a team which included archeologists, assistant surveyors and architects, a cartographer, an Egyptologist, and an inspector of antiquities from the Egyptian Antiquities Organisation. At different intervals of the project, his efforts were further supported by specialists: mining, structural, and electrical engineers, hydrologists, mechanics, and geologists. Without the contributions of others, the account reads differently.

My story would read differently, too, if not for the input and influence of a group of people. My achievements never happen without family, friends, and significant others—

namely, George Davis, my youth pastor in Rockaway, New Jersey, who believed I could be more than a troubled youth hanging out on a street corner; Ben Wikramanayake, my boss at Bank of America, who fostered my potential; Michelle Patterson, market leader of the downtown Los Angeles branch of Robert Half International, who identified transferable skills from my life in the ministry to the staffing industry; Enola Lipaz, who persuaded a team of CPAs to hire me, a noncredentialed sales guy, to help expand Resources Connection's market presence; Sandra Bensworth, my business partner, who called me and suggested we start our own accounting and finance consulting firm; and Joe Amella, CEO of Accretive Solutions, who acquired the business Sandra and I had built.

Most people can draw lines that connect the dots of their success to others—if they are willing. Some, out of hubris and a desire to be known as "self-made" men or women, choose not to. In his speech ironically entitled "Self-Made Men," Frederick Douglas affirms "there are in the world no such men as self-made men." We all benefit from someone or borrow something to become who we are and to get where we are. More on that later.

Achievements are not manufactured in a vacuum; whether credit is ascribed to them or not, others always play a part. We all need a helping hand at one time or another. "I didn't know what I was doing half the time. I nearly always had help," said Harry Potter to wizards learning how to defend themselves against Voldemort. And if a world-renowned wizard like Harry Potter needs help . . .

Here are some recognizable examples of those who received help along the way, whose accomplishments are affixed to others:

- Steve Jobs: the face of Apple. His genius
  manifested itself in how he handled the marketing
  side of the company. The credit for who conceived

a series of user-friendly computers, however, goes to Steve Wozniak. While Jobs paced numerous stages introducing Apple products, the company's incredible achievements would have never happened without the lesser-spotlighted Wozniak.

- The 1996 New York Yankees had a star-studded roster, which included Derek Jeter, Mariano Rivera, Jorge Posada, Bernie Williams, and Andy Pettitte—legends to those of us with an appreciation for baseball history, especially Yankee fans. But no one player can be credited with their World Series victory that year. Along with those noted above, other less glitzy personnel, like Paul O'Neill, Tino Martinez, Joe Girardi, and others, contributed to their championship win.

- The path-clearing work of John the Baptist, who preached a fervent message of repentance in the Judean Desert, preceded Jesus's inauguration. When Jesus hit the scene, he told the crowds who had gathered to listen to him that the following Old Testament passage was fulfilled in John: "I will send my messenger ahead of you, who will prepare your way before you" (Matthew 11:10). John paved the way for Jesus.

When you review the last five to ten years of your life, who comes to mind? Are you where you are today because they helped you in some way?

Have you noticed how certain phrases in the English language emphasize an interconnectedness between accomplishments and others? We say "standing on the shoulders of giants" to communicate that our own intellectual progress has been advanced because of the thought leaders who have preceded us. "To build a better mousetrap" is only to improve a version of an existing item. Rappers have a reputation of "biting" off the style of others to create their own technique. The tagline "Often imitated, never duplicated" is meant to suggest that others may copy a company's product but will never be as good as the original.

In his book *Where Good Ideas Come From: The Natural History of Innovation*, Steven Johnson tells readers that good ideas do not exist independent of the contribution and work of others: "Good ideas are not conjured out of thin air; they are built out of a collection of existing parts, the composition of which expands over time."[1] (Remember how I noted in chapter 2 that careers are a complex cluster of characteristics? It seems good ideas have the same makeup.)

A survey Johnson conducted revealed that scientists rarely, if ever, have a flash of inspiration, or eureka moment, alone in a lab. Rather, those insights occur while in communication with others, while sitting in a coffeehouse, for example. So, one scientist's success depends on that of another—he or she only builds on the work and research of those who have come before.

Only one original exists: what follows has been borrowed from what came first. Or as sagacious Solomon said, "What has been will be again, what has been done will be done again; there is nothing new under the sun" (Ecclesiastes 1:9). In other words, we all "bite" off others and will continue to do so for the foreseeable future.

Of course, there may be occasions you "go it alone." (The journey of every career hero begins with answering a call to tread a path no one else may follow.) In the movie *127 Hours*, James Franco portrays mountaineer and adventurer Aron Ralston, a person with no qualms about venturing out solo. While on one of his adventures, he gets trapped when a boulder falls on his arm and pins him against a canyon wall. Over a five-day span, he contemplates his life and considers his options to free himself. For days, nobody responds to his cries for help. He is left with one choice and decides to amputate his arm, a decision with pain points on several levels: physical, emotional, and psychological.

At times, those who pursue their calling feel trapped, stuck, as the saying goes, "between a rock and a hard place." They face moments when tough choices must be made—even the need to cut something off to survive. Joseph Campbell, mythologist and author of *The Hero With a Thousand Faces*, puts it this way: "Each who has dared to harken and follow the secret call has known the perils of the dangerous, solitary transit."[2]

There are some challenges that must be faced alone, but the "dangers" you face will likely never be as dramatic as Ralston's rock-climbing escapade. You will certainly find yourself in predicaments—spots that make you question what you are doing and why something is happening. Even still, when pinned and pressed in a difficult position, more often than not a helping hand can be found: family, friends, significant others, or those who specialize in career development, like recruiters, life coaches, and mentors.

In myth narratives, aid is afforded the hero who has answered the call to live an exceptional, destined life. Protective figures—fairy godmothers, wizards, and hermits, for example—provide the hero with advice, assurance, and amulets—jewelry that protects a person against evil, danger, and disease. These guardians tend to appear on one's journey —during desert wanderings, holy quests, and when navigating scary forests, dark caves, and terrifying tunnels.

The person working toward fulfilling his or her destiny only has to accept and believe that the ageless defenders will appear and provide protection. J.K. Rowling says something similar in *Harry Potter and the Deathly Hallows* but adds a qualifier: "Help will always be given at Hogwarts to those who ask for it."

The trick then is to recognize when help presents itself and accept it—or ask for it.

In the initial stages of building a career—when wearisome work seems to generate limited returns—day-in-and-day-out drudgery can be disheartening. But help always seems to come at opportune times and from various sources: a manager who offers practical on-the-job training; a customer who awards a contract to your fledgling start-up opposed to your competitor; a recruiter who identifies talents within you that you could not see in yourself; or a phone call from a parent or friend who offers a word of encouragement at just the right moment—a simple message that reminds you to keep digging because your discovery is a shovelful away.

And if help does not come? Ask for it. You will need it—obstacles *will* be encountered.

Jumper Cables

- Everyone desires to make their mark in the world, to have notable achievements and accomplishments.
- Whether someone is willing to admit it or not, their achievements and accomplishments happened because of the contribution of others: there are no self-made men or women.
- Here are a few accomplished people who have others to thank for their success: Steve Jobs, who relied on Steve Wozniak; the 1996 Yankees who won the world series that year because of the contributions of the whole team—not just the shining stars; and Jesus, whose ministry benefitted from the path-clearing efforts of John the Baptist. Think about the successful people you know and ask them to tell you about who helped them to get where they are.
- Take some time to think about who has helped

you so far in your career. Send them a thank-you card to express your appreciation for their contribution to your career development.

- Remember: there can only be one original. The rest of us, at on one level or another, are copycats. Your success is connected to the success of someone else.
- Help will always come to those who pursue their calling. The trick is to recognize when it presents itself and accept it when it is offered. If that does not happen, ask for it. You will be surprised at how many people are willing to offer a helping hand.

6 DOORS FIRST, THEN DISCOVERIES: EXPECT OBSTACLES

EXCAVATIONS ARE NOT WITHOUT CHALLENGES. THEY ARE no walk in the park, as they say—or a leisurely stroll around Egypt's desert. Dr. Weeks and his team faced many difficulties —geological struggles, engineering troubles, political red tape, and standard archeological structural challenges. At the onset of your career, you will also come across a plethora of problems that prevent passage and progress to your discovery. You cannot get around them; you must work through them.

At a certain point in their excavation, Dr. Weeks and his team came face-to-face with their obstacle: a stone door at the end of a long corridor. According to Michael Lemonick's *Time* magazine cover story from May 1995, they faced a door that had been "blocked for thousands of years."[1] To pry it open would be a labor-intensive task for any mindful archeologist. But if they did, an amazing discovery waited on the other side of it, the burial chambers of Ramesses II's family, the largest tomb ever discovered in that part of Egypt.

Before Jesus raised his friend Lazarus from the dead, he told those standing at the entrance of the burial tomb, "Take away the stone" (John 11:39). Afraid the smell from the decaying corpse might overwhelm him, the group admonished

Jesus not to bother—Lazarus was good and dead. (The biblical account says he had already been in the tomb four days.) Jesus assured them Lazarus lived; he was only sleeping. In other words, he asked them to have faith. Once they removed the stone, Lazarus—who was wrapped in burial clothes and looked like a mummy—exited the chamber.

Not that I am comparing Dr. Weeks to Jesus, but in both scenarios, massive stones blocked discoveries—on the one hand, proof of an ancient civilization buried thousands of years ago, and on the other, proof that God can raise people from the dead.

If you do not remove the obstructions you encounter, what will others fail to see? Getting on the other side of your obstacle benefits more than yourself.

But not all "stones" you deal with will be big. Most are puny, like the ones that end up in your shoe—pestering pebbles that prevent pain-free progress but are a pain in your ass. Some stop their excavations because of those pebbles.

Safe to say, archeologists get little stones in their shoes, or in the least, some sand, a looser, more granular form of rock. It goes with the territory. But you do not need to be on an excavation to get a proverbial pebble in your proverbial shoe.

Average, run-of-the-mill employees find them in their shoes all the time: favoritism, racism, chauvinism, ageism, wage inequality, sexism, and managerial incompetence, to name some—a variety of "pebbles" that hamper advancement toward discoveries. Life's pebbles also find their way into our shoes, but that is a list too long to note here. As with any pebble in a shoe, your foot will let you know about it, and when it does, you will agree—it is a real pain in the patootie.

You will encounter lots of pains in the ass at work: managers who "crack the whip" like Indiana Jones; coworkers who, like marauders stealing relics at an archeological site, take credit for your work; and competitors who would prefer to bury you in a tomb rather than help you, let alone resurrect you.

As my first entrepreneurial venture blossomed, I learned one of my competitors placed me on a hush-hush intraoffice Most Hated List, an honor in which I still take pride—a certain amount of pleasure is derived from being a pebble in someone else's shoe. Some professionals just don't know how to "play nice in the sandbox"—get used to it. And there will always be someone "throwing stones." Do your best to stay out of harm's way because sticks and stones can break your bones. Just be sure to tell those stone throwers to go "pound sand," which, if you don't know, is a much nicer way of saying, "Fuck off."

Consider obstacles—no matter what form they may take —to be confirmation that you are onto something. You are heading in the right direction. You are getting closer to your discovery.

One of the main obstacles you will face at the beginning of your career is this: your unwillingness to take ownership of your life of employment. There will be occasions you feel tempted to blame someone or something for your lack of progress.

By now, you may have noticed my fondness for folklore, stories that teach us about our humanity and make poignantly clear the foibles of humankind. The myth of Orestes, for example, is quite instructive on the matter of "owning up," or accepting responsibility for your actions. The following details the sequence of events in the story:

- Orestes was the grandson of Artreus, who in his arrogance tried to prove himself stronger than the gods.
- The gods punished Artreus for this and cursed his descendants, including Clytemnestra, Orestes's mother.

- As part of the enactment of this curse, Clytemnestra killed her husband, Orestes's father.
- This created a dilemma for Orestes: he must now kill his mother to fulfill an obligation to honor a Greek code that demanded his father's murderer be killed. The only problem: the greatest sin a Greek could commit was the sin of matricide, killing one's mother. If you killed your mother, you were destined to live a cursed life.
- Orestes agonized over his dilemma but ultimately decided to do what he had to do and killed his mother.
- The gods punished him for this sin and sent the Furies, creatures with the head and body of a woman and a bird's wings and talons, who tormented and clawed at him. (Interestingly, only Orestes could see and hear them.)
- After years of reflection and self-loathing, Orestes petitioned the gods to remove the curse.
- The gods held a trial. Apollo, Olympian god of the sun, light, music, and everything beautiful, defended Orestes, letting the tribunal know he himself orchestrated the whole situation and, thus, Orestes should not be held liable—he had no choice but to kill his mother.
- Despite Apollo's confession, Orestes, who accepted the crummy hand he had been dealt, still told the gods he was responsible for all that happened.
- The gods, shocked because they had never seen anyone take total responsibility for their actions, relented and reversed the curse, and the Furies were transformed into Eumenides, benign spirits who sent good fortune to Orestes.

If I were Orestes, I would ask myself, "How in the world

did I end up here?" and "Why am I in the spot I am in?" and "Why did this happen to me?" But here's the thing: he did not blame his family, even though he could have pointed his finger at his grandfather, and he did not blame the gods or "fate" for the terrible torments that came his way, even though Apollo admitted he'd had a hand in Orestes's misfortune. Instead, he accepted his reality, petitioned for help, and sought a solution to what most would call a shitty situation.

Work really sucks sometimes, especially when you are in the infancy stages of your career, when you are "paying your dues." Rest assured, you will have ample reasons to blame others and "curse the gods" for the troubles and hardships that come your way: those who say you are not qualified for the job; those who do not value your contribution to the organization; mean-hearted managers who berate you; backstabbing coworkers; a corporate transaction that moves your job overseas; or a merger or acquisition that eliminates your job. You can add to this list daily: most workdays bring a reason or two as to why your butt would hurt.

Many never find their calling because they refuse to push past the rubble, dirt, and waste that must be cleared away. Their discovery lies on the other side of the door, but they are unwilling to do what has to be done to get beyond it. Instead, martyr-like reasons occupy their thoughts. Maybe you have heard them carp:

- "I can't catch a break. Nothing ever goes my way. It's like a black cloud is hanging over my head."
- "I have limited connections, limited education, and limited talent."
- "I am too young and lack experience." (Later these turn into "I'm too old and have too much experience.")
- "I will never make it. I am destined to fail." (The epitome of negative self-talk.)

- "My employer does not value me."
- "Things would be different if I didn't get screwed over."
- "Some have all the luck. Not me."
- "I got downsized . . . again."

The story of Orestes, however, tells you to refuse to make excuses or participate in the blame game. Pointing the finger at people and problems prevents progress: it postpones finding your calling; it pushes the pause button on becoming who you are meant to be; and it puts on the backburner what you are meant to accomplish. You cannot dodge real-life self-growth opportunities and self-responsibility and still expect to advance toward your discovery, the treasure which lies on the other side of your obstacle.

Did you notice that the Furies were transformed into Eumenides only *after* Orestes accepted responsibility for all that happened to him? You can bitch and whine all you want about your lot in life, how things never go your way, and who did this or that to you. Maybe you need a moment to get it out of your system. Alright. Granted. Take your moment. When you are done, take ownership for anything and everything that has come your way. Then the curses will become blessings.

Jumper Cables

- Careers and callings are not without challenges: you are bound to encounter obstacles.
- Dr. Weeks and his team removed dirt, rubble, and more before finding the door that blocked their discovery. List five things you would define as rubble.

- List on a piece of paper the "pebbles" in your shoe that hinder your advancement.
- Think about the excuses you make and how often you point the finger at people and circumstances. What can you do to change your situation in life?
- The next time you face a challenge, take the time to list five potential solutions. Don't bother thinking about who's to blame.
- Remember: obstacles confirm you are heading in the right direction.
- The tale of Orestes conveys the importance of accepting responsibility. Taking ownership is the precursor to curses becoming blessings.

7 THE IMPORTANCE OF TIME

ONE OF THE GREATEST BLESSINGS YOU HAVE BEEN GIVEN is time.

When you are young, you think you have a never-ending supply of it, and you spend it liberally. When you are old, you look to buy back as much of it as you can. Most of us assume we have more of it than we do and waste more of it than we should.

As I picked through the story of Dr. Weeks, I found another piece of ancient wisdom for those about to enter the workforce: do not waste time but do not rush either.

My wife chides me about my tendency to rush. "Not everything has to be the Amazing Race," she says. If asked, she will tell you that she hates going to the airport with me. That is because on those days, I channel Flash Gordon, who, as comic book aficionados know, runs at the superfast speed of 2,532 miles per hour.

Here is what a trip to the airport looks like for us: I push us out of the house, force us into the car, and then speed down California's freeways in a quest to set a world record. Once inside the airport, I shove us through the check-in process. Next, I drag us to the TSA inspection area where we remove apparel and accessories. After we re-adorn ourselves, I propel us toward the boarding gate, where, now seated, I fidget.

As soon as the gate attendant calls the first boarding group, I get in line ASAP, even if my group number has not yet been called. After the attendant scans my boarding pass, I hightail it through the tunnel, leaving my wife in the dust, only to be frustrated by the reality of another line.

My impatience grows as I shimmy down the aisle of the plane, balancing my two carry-ons. I am baffled and annoyed that it takes forever and a day for folks to put their travel bags in the overhead bins. Edginess and intensity grip me from the time we leave our home to the time I find my seat on the plane. It takes being rooted to my assigned spot for me to relax.

My best guess as to why I get like this is that I like reaching logical conclusions. It seems simple to me: if one must fly, then one must be in a seat on a plane; the sooner you get in that seat, the sooner the plane takes off and the sooner you hear the pilot utter those wonderful words, "We have reached our destination."

All this to say, we sometimes approach our career like I approach getting to and going through an airport. We rush to destination points, one position after another, as we climb up the corporate ladder as quickly as possible, while a career metronome clicks back and forth in our minds to mark the time.

If you are anything like me, you want to get where you are going as soon as possible; this includes getting *somewhere* career-wise. But careers, like most things that improve over time, develop at a less rapid rate: time is on your side, whether you know it or not. You are not in the Amazing Race. Sometimes I think to myself I should just slow down—running and racing toward some "destination" makes me feel like I am on the proverbial hamster wheel.

By "slow," however, I mean step-by-step movement toward

a goal—at an archeologist's pace, not a Flash Gordon pace. Archeologists never rush; speed is unimportant. They dig, remove debris, and clear tunnels for years—countless hours are spent searching for indications of the ancient civilizations they seek. Methodical and systematic in approach, archeologists like Dr. Weeks measure success not by how quick but by how careful things are done.

His year-in-year-out work on the elaborate system of tunnels below the earth's surface begs us to slow down. It recommends a speed strange to most of us, a slower stride we struggle to imagine that can lead to significant accomplishments. (For the record, Dr. Weeks began his project in 1979 and did not make his grand discovery until 1989.) His course of action reminds me of the Chinese proverb that says, "Be not afraid of growing slowly; be afraid of only standing still."

Maybe a few examples of those who moved at a slower pace will help you understand what I mean:

- Early on, Walt Disney developed an interest in drawing. He took art classes, got a job as a commercial illustrator at eighteen, and faced different challenges as he explored the world of animation. *Alice's Wonderland,* as it was originally known, struggled to make money, and it was not until *Steamboat Willie,* almost ten years later, that things began to look up. Everything evolved from there, and the rest is history, as they say. All these years later, Walt's message to all admirers of the kingdom he built over time is still clear: "Always remember that this whole thing was started with a dream and a mouse." Over the span of many years, the happiest place on Earth grew into the enormous conglomerate it is today.
- After college, Joanne Rowling started her career as a temporary employee and took jobs as a bilingual

secretary. In 1990 the idea for a children's fantasy series came to her as she waited on a delayed train. (It is not uncommon for careers to feel delayed, or dormant for a period of time.) Before she published, she got married, had a daughter, relocated to Scotland after her divorce, and lived on state assistance, while she wrote. Publication for the *Harry Potter* series commenced in 1997 and continued through 2007. Five hundred million copies of the series have been sold, and her books have been translated into seventy languages. In 2008 Rowling was named the highest-paid author by *Forbes* magazine.

- Most people know the background story of the making of *Jaws*. The project, which was supposed to take fifty-five days to produce, ended up taking 159 days. The delays resulted from a bunch of production nightmares: actors that feuded, props that malfunctioned, a budget that skyrocketed from $3.5 million to $9 million, boats that sank, extras that became disgruntled, and scripts that needed to be rewritten. A lot was on the line for Steven Spielberg: the making of this film could sink or make his career. As we know, the pieces fell into place, and the movie went on to be a huge success. A masterpiece that took longer to create than was planned has generated worldwide box office sales of $472 million.

Background stories like this are great because they contextualize the success of others and let us know the time it took and the effort exerted to achieve it. Unobstructed paths to success do not exist, and it takes time to clear the rubble-strewn roads that lead to your accomplishments.

Slower speeds and measured movements should not be

confused with inactivity. "Though you be swift as the wind, I will beat you in a race," said the Tortoise to the Hare. Aesop's quaint tale is a reminder of the ever-important moral of a "slow but steady pace," a concept that may be hard for those who live in a fast-paced, digitized world to accept.

The story of the Tortoise and the Hare as well as the lives of Disney, Rowling, Spielberg, and Dr. Weeks run counter to today's tempo. Rarely, if ever, is someone an "overnight success." It may seem so because, when these success stories are told, the individual is presented in the glory of morning light, after they have achieved something. They appear untouched by the hardships experienced along the way. Their magazine images are glossy. The reality: much time was spent working their way toward the pinnacle they are now perched upon.

In a *New Yorker* article entitled "How Bernardine Evaristo Conquered British Literature," Evaristo is quoted for joking about being an "'overnight success' . . . only four decades in the making."[1] For years Evaristo was kept from the corridors of Britain's literary power and the respect afforded those who walked those halls. She struggled to break in and spent years, as Canadian poet Margaret Atwood said of her, "toiling in the salt mines of literature." In other words, she worked hard to remove the dirt and debris of British literary prejudice.

We prefer to look at our heroes of success after they shower off the shit they had to wade through: Walt Disney dressed in a suit looking executive-like in his corporate office, Stephen Spielberg wearing a tuxedo at the Oscars, J.K. Rowling being appointed a member of the Order of the Companions of Honour for her services in literature and philanthropy, and Dr. Weeks lecturing in academic lecture halls. We prefer the shine and sheen of a presumed overnight success over the lackluster look of the laborer.

That type of thinking—that you should go "from rags to riches" without "blood, sweat, and tears"—devalues the importance of time. Not knowing how much time we have, we should waste none of it. Work your ass off like you want to get where you are going as quickly as possible—wherever that may be—but do not rush either. Let time work its magic, and do not skip over the hard work and tedious tasks that clear the path for you to find—and appreciate—your discovery.

Jumper Cables

- Everyone has been given the blessing of time; how much of it we have, we do not know. Do not assume you have more of it than you do, and do not waste what time you have been given.
- Think about how you use your time. How productive are you with your work hours? Are they spent trying to fulfill your calling?
- You are not in the Amazing Race. Remember: careers develop at a rate slower than you might like. Try not to measure your career by how quickly you reach a certain position within an organization. If you are rushing your career, learn to adopt a longer-term perspective.
- Review the backstories of Walt Disney, J.K. Rowling, and Steven Spielberg, and note the similarities between them.
- Drive to your favorite restaurant, but do not take the freeway; use side streets. See if you find that more enjoyable than taking the freeway.
- Moving at a slow pace is not inactivity. You will get where you are going if you keep moving forward. Next time you sit on your couch for two hours straight, get up and say to yourself, "Now that's inactivity."

8 THE UNIQUENESS OF YOU

OVER THE YEARS, MANY NOTEWORTHY DISCOVERIES HAVE been made by different archeologists: Pierre-François Bouchard discovered the Rosetta Stone; Victor Loret found Amenhotep's mummy; Ernesto Schiaparelli located the tomb of Nefertari; and Howard Carter came upon the tomb of King Tutankhamun. Their maps, their excavation work, and their discoveries had distinction; each was *sui generis*, unlike that of another. Likewise, the same can be said about Dr. Weeks: his maps, his excavation, and his discoveries were without equal. And the same should be said about your endeavors, no matter what career you choose to pursue.

Much of what I have written—finding the overarching theme of *your* career; drawing a map to outline the place to begin to excavate for *your* career; making time for mysticism to hear messages that guide *your* career; taking ownership of *your* life of employment; using *your* time wisely to build *your* career —all is aimed at getting you to personalize what you plan to do with the next forty to fifty years of *your* life. That time should reflect your uniqueness as a person. As Oscar Wilde, renowned author famous for his unconventional approach to life *and* writing, has said, "Be yourself; everyone else is taken."

Quentin Crisp, writer and humorist known for his flamboyance, echoed the same sentiment when he said something similar in his book *How to Have a Lifestyle*: "In the end you have only one thing to offer the world that no one else can give, and that is yourself." So, I say: never choose an occupation that does not allow *you* to be part of the equation. Any job that asks you to divorce yourself from the job you do is not the job for you.

Easier said than done, some might say. Today's workplace seems to prize uniformity over individuality. True. The shadows cast by megacorporations and conglomerates loom large and make it difficult to be distinct, to stand out among your peers. Companies do this because uniformity of staff eliminates complexity: people are easier to manage when an indistinguishable sameness characterizes them.

Lately there has been a push by companies to improve their approach. Counterintuitive thoughts and alternative views and approaches are a bit more welcomed. Executives have started to listen to the voices of the "unlike" and "different." Some corporations have realized a complex workforce—the strands represented by a diverse employee base—make an organization stronger, not weaker.

But old ways die hard, and many places of employment still prefer hiring employees cut from the same cloth—employees who, at least on paper, look the same. The thinking goes like this: those who "think outside the box" and those unwilling to "toe the line" can infect an organization, and infections must be eradicated immediately. More specifically, the person spreading the ailment should be dismissed as quickly as possible, before his or her dissimilar thoughts spread to the entire workforce.

For the system to function optimally—for top- and bottom-line revenue targets to be met—everyone must stick to the program and work in a regimented Borg-like fashion, as if part of the Collective. In a lecture series from the 1950s,

Aldous Huxley warns about organizations that "deindividualize" people to make them fit into the company.[1] Sadly, companies like this still exist and choose to leave little room for peculiarity.

You probably know people who, at one time or another, felt like a stranger in a strange land: a coworker or manager who comes across as different from the rest, a teacher who has his or her own style, or a coach with an unorthodox approach. Being unlike others can make you feel that way, like you are an outsider, like you don't fit in. Here is a pair of notable characters who felt this way:

- The maker of myths, Stan Lee: when Lee started out, the zeitgeist of the time was negative toward comic books and those who produced them. (Fredric Wertham, a Bavarian-born psychiatrist and disciple of Freud, embarked on an anticomics crusade, saying there was a correlation between juvenile delinquency and avid readers of comics.)

At the same time, comic book companies struggled to produce and make a profit from them. In light of this antagonistic spirit, Lee wondered if his out-of-the-ordinary ideas made any sense.

To start, he had an atypical view of what a superhero should be. To him, superheroes were not infallible; they should be more like you and me, with one caveat: they possessed supernatural powers. Their flaws, he thought, should be highlighted as much as their powers.

In his book *Stan Lee: A Life in Comics,* Liel Leibovitz tells us Lee wanted his superheroes to be like the heroes he admired: Sherlock Holmes, a druggie detective with an addiction; Quasimodo, a hunchback hell-bent on homicide; and Hamlet, Denmark's prince, who was ravenous for revenge. In a nutshell, Lee wanted his heroes to be superhuman but human nonetheless.[2]

Secondly, he had different opinions on how the comic itself should be created. At the time, artisans—the writers, the pencilers, the inkers, and the colorists—were pigeonholed in their roles and only focused on those roles, nothing more. Lee preferred a method that allowed the worker to freestyle. His employees had more freedom to put themselves into their work.

Someone who values their own individuality always promotes it in others.

- By 1995, Howard Stern really came into his own, but his uniqueness was evident from an early age. Like Dr. Weeks, he always knew what he wanted to be—in his case, an American radio personality. At a young age, his father even set up a microphone, tape machine, and turntable so Howard could channel his creativity and produce make-believe shows.

When his career started, he bounced from station to station, mainly because he did not fit in: his style of humor did not fly with more conservative station owners or managers. To see how his idiosyncratic approach bugged the crap out of his superiors at WNBC, watch his movie, *Private Parts*.

Regardless, Howard's popularity with his audience grew, despite attempts by NBC's executives to control him. His style could not be restrained. Encouraged by Stern's unconventional behavior, his coworkers—Robin Quivers, Gary "Baba Booey" Dell'Abate, and Fred Norris—followed suit and added their own brand of quirkiness to the show.

The uniqueness of Lee and Stern shined bright, in part, because the background they stood in front of was dark. Oftentimes a difficult environment becomes the milieu in which your uniqueness—and your career—can flourish. Negative backdrops and challenging work environments offer a platform whereby you can stand out in a distinct way.

Take, for example, Itzchak Tarkay, acrylic painter and watercolorist extraordinaire. At the age of nine, he and his family were sent to the Mauthausen concentration camp, heartlessly hauled away to remote killing fields, like so many others, where dreams were dark, hopes faded into a black abyss, and lives were snuffed out like a candle's light. He and his family happened to be on "the list" of those to be exterminated, even though the existence of a "list" never entered their minds.

After being liberated by Allied forces in 1949—when light finally broke through the darkness—he immigrated to Israel, received a scholarship to the Avni Art Academy, and learned from well-known Israeli artists of the time. Influenced by French Impressionists and Post-Impressionists like Matisse and Toulouse-Lautrec, Tarkay's art focused on dream-like images of elegant women, perhaps in reaction to the heart-wrenching images he saw at Mauthausen.

His paintings juxtapose and layer colors; tones bleed into each other in an atypical way and create vibrant shades for the backgrounds, clothing, faces, and even the eyeshadow colors of the females he brings to life on canvas. Despite years staring into the charcoal-colored chasm of a concentration camp, he still envisioned spectrums of color; he still found a kaleidoscope of hues from which to paint.

He defied the blackness of this backdrop and let the radiant colors he envisioned splash onto tarps that waited to be touched by the brush held by the hand of his soul. The darkness of his experience helped him define the nuances of his distinct persona and his career in the world of art. For such a virtuoso, his moniker as the "magician with color," could not have been more apt.

Expect the initial phases of your career to have challenges.

Typically, it is a time of training and development; long hours are spent learning about the job, including what to do and what not to do. When I started in the staffing industry, my training included my manager sitting next to me as I made one cold call after another, each followed by a discussion on what I had done right and what I could have done better. Those were long twelve-hour days. But that time allowed me to cultivate my own style and develop a business acumen that prepared me for broader business conversations I would have later in my career with countless managers, supervisors, and executives.

The beginning phase of your career—which somewhat corresponds to the time you transition from adolescence to adulthood—is a great time to refine who you want to be and what you what to do, from a work standpoint, with your life.

There are those who have all this sorted out prior to their first work experience, as the lives of Dr. Weeks and Howard Stern attest. For many, maybe even most, however, it takes a while; a discovery or two made along the way helps them redefine their map—and that is okay. At the end of the day, you are just trying to be the best version of yourself. The important thing is to allow your true self to make it onto the canvas of your career.

Jumper Cables

- Noteworthy discoveries have been made over the years by different archeologists, but each had distinction. Likewise, your life of employment should reflect your uniqueness. Pick a career that allows you to be your true self.
- To build a career unlike others, you must personalize it.

- If a job does not allow you to be you, then it is not the job for you.
- Ask yourself if your current work environment values individuality over uniformity. If it does not, it may be time to amend your map and figure out how to transition to an employer who values that.
- Make a list of people you know who are unorthodox. What do you like about their style?
- Look up the etymology of the word *unique*. List three synonyms of the word *unique*, and think about how you can reflect that uniqueness in a work environment.
- Remember: negative backdrops provide opportunities for your uniqueness to shine.
- Review the stories of Stan Lee, Howard Stern, and Itzchak Tarkay. What about their approaches would be good to emulate?

9 LET YOUR WORK SPEAK FOR ITSELF

Dr. Weeks made an amazing discovery. Other archeologists made discoveries, too, but KV5 was the largest burial site ever found in Egypt. His work uncovered an enormous amount about ancient Egypt and its most famous king, Ramesses II. As mentioned, what he did drew worldwide attention. His *project* was featured in a best-selling issue of *Time* magazine.

But Dr. Weeks accomplished more than the discovery itself. He conducted a comprehensive survey of the tombs and monuments of the West Bank at Luxor and created a catalog of the archeological remains found by him and his team, launched the Theban Mapping Project website, introduced the use of hot air balloons to take aerial photos of the territory he explored, and published the *Atlas of the Valley of the Kings*, a collection of seventy-two sheets of maps and tomb plans.

And all this was done without drawing attention to himself. Sure, part of his job required him to make statements on behalf of the American University in Cairo about the work he and his team accomplished along the way. But he never pointed to himself in a way that said, "Look at me!" or "Look what I did!" His work spoke for itself.

Rod Tidwell, fictional football player played by Cuba Gooding Jr. in *Jerry Maguire*, is a self-promoting, where's-my-big-contract?, "show me the money" type. After Jerry Maguire, played by Tom Cruise, gets fired from Sports Management International (SMI), Rod, who is difficult to please, ends up being his one and only client.

Rod thinks Jerry is not trying hard enough to get him his big contract as well as the endorsements that provide alternative streams of income. Jerry, on the other hand, thinks Rod is not yet worthy of all he hopes to get and thinks he deserves; he thinks Rod still has to prove himself.

Later in the movie, during a game on *Monday Night Football*, Rod makes a game-winning catch in dramatic fashion. (He lands on his neck and goes unconscious for a period of time but ends up being fine.) Unbeknownst to Rod, Jerry had secured an $11.2 million contract, which would allow Rod to play football in his home state of Arizona, where he also played college football as a Sun Devil. Rod finally received the money—and the accolades—he felt he deserved for his efforts.

A hard lesson to learn but one that must be learned—one best learned at the start of your career and one Dr. Weeks epitomized—is to let your work validate itself. An achievement is its own reward.

That said, everyone, like Rod Tidwell, likes to be praised and rewarded for a job well done. And there is nothing wrong with that. Sam Walton, American businessman and entrepreneur who founded Walmart and Sam's Club, gets at how important praise is in his essay entitled "Running a Successful Company: Ten Rules that Worked for Me": "Nothing else can quite substitute for a few well-chosen, well-timed, sincere words of praise."

Even children evidence a need to be praised for something they have done. Studies show that praise boosts good feelings, increases motivation, and inspires us to be more hardworking. When a child—or anyone, for that matter—hears, "Wow!

Great job!" or gets a high five from someone who has recognized what they have done, their behavior is reinforced, and they are invigorated to keep at it. It just goes to show we all appreciate a pat on the back for a job well done.

There is no doubt about it: accomplishments should be acknowledged, even celebrated. When I close a business deal, I celebrate with room-temperature cheese, RITZ crackers, and an icy cold libation—whether my achievements have been acknowledged or not.

It is a sad but true fact that many employers miss opportunities to praise and celebrate an employee's accomplishments. Do not be surprised if that is your experience.

Regardless, praise is best when it comes unsolicited. To ask for it is to diminish its value; it creates discordant clamor, like an old, noisy muffler on a high-performance vehicle. Better to wait for someone to say something than to spell it out for them.

What is the point if you have to point it out for it to be pointed out?

An Austro-Bohemian Romantic composer and one of the leading conductors of his generation, Gustav Mahler is known as someone whose music bridged nineteenth-century Austro-German tradition with the modernism of the early twentieth century. He is also known for full-sounding compositions— bold, in-your-face music that does not overwhelm listeners by being loud. His music proves you can produce vast volume without making loud, clangy sounds. If your work is done well, it will speak volumes—clash and crash cymbals and big bass drums will not be needed to draw someone's attention to it.

Do not be concerned with getting credit for what you have done; be concerned with getting more done—rewards will take care of themselves.

It takes humility not to yell out the reasons why you feel you deserve to be recognized. There will be times you want to scream out that you should get a bigger bonus, a promotion, or some sort of reward for your labor. While you may feel justified in these feelings, it is still best to let the work speak for itself.

One way you can keep a lid on these noisy outbursts is to remember you are part of an organization, part of a team. And, as I said in an earlier chapter, achievements are seldom solo efforts: someone else always plays a role in your accomplishments.

To keep yourself in check from a humility standpoint, Bill Parcells, legendary football coach who won championships with the New England Patriots and the New York Giants, recommends putting the spotlight on the team over individual efforts. Teams are judged by how many victories they have won, not by the individual statistics you can find on the back of a sports card.

While your individual stats may be great, humility says there is always room for improvement. In his book *Finding A Way To Win*, Parcells advises, "The instant you relax, or drop off, or rely on *who* you are rather than *what* you're doing, you're on the express lane to the chopping block."[1] In other words, no one is indispensable. If the CEO of an organization can be fired, so can you.

Saxon White Kessinger wrote an old-fashioned piece of poetry called "Indispensable Man" about this very thing. It deserves to be included here in its entirety:

Sometime when you're feeling important;
Sometime when your ego's in bloom
Sometime when you take it for granted
You're the best qualified in the room,

Sometime when you feel that your going
Would leave an unfillable hole,
Just follow these simple instructions

And see how they humble your soul;

Take a bucket and fill it with water,
Put your hand in it up to the wrist,
Pull it out and the hole that's remaining
Is a measure of how you'll be missed.

You can splash all you wish when you enter,
You may stir up the water galore,
But stop and you'll find that in no time
It looks quite the same as before.

The moral of this quaint example
Is do just the best you can,
Be proud of yourself but remember,
There's no indispensable man.[2]

A friend of mine had a good run with his employer and lived at the top of the sales scorecard five years straight. He never had a quarter where his revenue production dipped below what it was the quarter before. The money he generated for the company rose quarter after quarter, year after year. He made them millions.

Strangely, his commissions dropped. Management cited a couple of reasons for this strange occurrence: "There are more mouths to feed" (the wealth needed to be shared with new employees added to the team), and "The bonus pool gets divvied up evenly amongst the team members" (actually, 75 percent was equally dispersed among the team, and the remaining 25 percent was allocated based on "managerial discretion"). Every year he worked hard to improve his performance and hoped it would translate into more personal earnings. The tact management took with him made him feel unappreciated and undervalued.

In private, he discussed the matter with his supervisor and

asked what more he could do to ensure better commissions. Her response did not satisfy. So, he had a decision to make: stay and live with a level of dissatisfaction in regard to the organization's compensation model, or leave and find an employer who rewarded their employees better. He left.

Since he was a top performer, he assumed the company might suffer in his absence; that did not happen. Market conditions and new hires continued to propel their business to new heights. Some might even say the company performed better in his absence. My friend went on to establish a business of his own so he could better control how rewards were doled out to himself and others. Objectively speaking, his decision to move on was a good one. Over the next year, he made more money than he did the prior three years with his former employer.

In general, it is always best to let your work speak for itself. No one likes a person who boasts about their accomplishments and demands praise for what they have done. True, the squeaky wheel gets the oil. But I have never met anyone who likes those who squeak.

There may be times you find yourself in a situation in which the accolades and acclaim never come, when your employer fails to seize any and all opportunities to acknowledge, in one way or another, what you have done for the company. In those instances, you must, like my friend, take matters into your own hands.

Jumper Cables

- Does your employer praise their employees for their accomplishments? Does your manager liberally commend those who work hard, those who get things done?
- Make sure you know how the company you work

for rewards its employees. Are there annual bonuses? Is your commission plan based on revenue generation or other performance indicators? Do you know the specifics about your compensation plan?

- Do not be concerned with getting credit for what you have done; be concerned with getting more done: rewards will take care of themselves.
- Keep a running list of all you think you have accomplished for your organization. Bring that with you when you have your performance review.
- Accomplishments should be acknowledged and celebrated. List three ways to celebrate yours.
- As much as you may accomplish, it is wise to remember achievements are seldom solo efforts. Next time you do a great job on something, think about who helped you and tell them thanks.
- Humility dictates we remember no one is indispensable. Everyone can be replaced, and the company you work for can and will carry on without you.
- Sometimes you have to take matters into your own hands. If your employer never rewards you for your efforts, it may be time to look for another job.

10 THE BOTTOM IS AS GOOD A PLACE AS ANY TO START

Fame came to Dr. Weeks after years of hard work. He began with study and devoted hours of time and attention to acquiring knowledge in archeology and anthropology. To boot, he minored in medicine and studied Greek and German. The rigors of study were then followed by the hardships of time in the field and years of hot sun and labor-intensive work. After all, archeology is, first and foremost, manual labor.

Other duties of an archeologist include research and assessments of past societies and cultures, testing theories about the origin and development of bygone cultures, and writing, presenting, and publishing reports regarding their findings—what some may call the more glamorous aspects of the job. Still, archeology mainly involves work with your hands—a day of shoveling dirt that leaves something under your fingernails. While commencing a dig is exciting, eventually it degenerates into moving earth one shovelful at a time and brushing sand off an ancient relic found. If you want to make a discovery, work like this must be done.

Not everyone has the opportunity to pursue an extensive education like Dr. Weeks, but when it comes to work, everyone can start somewhere, and there is no better place to start than the bottom.

If you start at the bottom, you will learn all you need to know to be at the top.

Vintners are an interesting crop of people who are part of an industry that, to many, is romantic. People tend to overly romanticize what owning a vineyard is like. They think to themselves, *What could be better than casually walking through the vineyard or sitting in a chateau with a glass of wine in your hand.* What they fail to see is the back-breaking gardening that must be done before that wine gets to the glass.

Most vintners first get a degree in viticulture and learn about grapes, growing regions, and local production and marketing regulations. Vintners, also known as enologists, oversee the entire winemaking process, from planting vines to harvesting and crushing the grapes, through the fermentation and aging process and then bottling. Like the really good archeologists who end up with dirt and dust on their clothes from their labors, the really good winemakers get their hands dirty, too, as they toil side by side with their workers throughout the winemaking stages.

Degreed or not, it is recommended that aspiring vintners learn the aspects of the job by starting as a cellar assistant, a "lower-level" job that requires you to clean and sanitize all cellar and bottling equipment, and whereby you gain knowledge of all wine pumps and harvest equipment and how they work. Time in the cellar, the reasoning goes, prepares you for time in the field, and both prepare you to influence the wine you produce, and appreciate the fruit of your labors.

The experience in the cellar—and the field—shapes the character of the laborer. The decisions you learn to make there influence the flavor profile of the wine you produce. Simply put, the wine you produce is an extension of who you have become in the cellar and the field.

When you enter the workforce for the first time, you

should expect to start at the ground floor. Dream and desire all you want about sitting in the corner office on the executive floor or about being the "top dog"; there is nothing wrong with that. But remember, you have to start somewhere, and more than likely, that will be an entry-level position.

Every job starts that way, no matter what industry you select. They all have rungs you must climb to get to the top. Seldom does someone start there on day one, though exceptions exist. Some have meteoric rises to the summit, and others are beneficiaries of family wealth that catapult them to their place of prominence within an organization. Most, like you and me, are not that lucky. So we start at the bottom and, through persistence and perseverance, make our way to higher ground. More common are the stories about those who accept preliminary, low-wage jobs and then work their way up the food chain.

Someone who knows a thing or two about food chains is Bobby Flay, successful restaurateur who branched out into TV in 1994 when he appeared on the Food Network's *Iron Chef America*. A couple years later, he starred in *Grillin' & Chillin'*, and then went on to shows like *Beat Bobby Flay*, *Brunch @ Bobby's*, and *Throwdown with Bobby Flay*. You would be wrong, however, to think Bobby did not first pay his dues as dishwasher, line cook, and sous chef.

After he dropped out of high school at seventeen, Flay took a job at Joe Allen's, a popular restaurant in New York's Theater District, where his job included making salads. In the introduction to *Bobby Flay's Mesa Grill Cookbook*, he notes that it was here, while "cranking out countless meals," that he dreamed of the restaurant concept for Mesa Grill.[1]

Luckily, Bobby's boss at Joe Allen's noticed something special about him and paid for him to attend New York City's French Culinary Institute. After culinary school, he worked several jobs learning what is was *really* like working in the kitchen of a restaurant.

But Bobby realized he was not ready to run a kitchen. As he says in his cookbook, "It was all fine and good to dream big, but I needed the skills first. I had no culinary point of view of my own yet."[2] And so he took a job as chef—not executive chef—at Bud's, owned by Jonathan Waxman, who introduced him to his now trademark southwestern-style flavors.

The rest is history, as they say. Bobby Flay has amassed a culinary empire that encompasses restaurants, TV shows, and cookbooks. His example shows that it takes maturity to pass up the top spot to hone your skills. Spotlights can equally show what you have *and* what you lack.

But Flay's experience, like that of others with dreams the size of California and even dreams you may have, reflects typical career progression, a step-by-step climb from the bottom to the top. We only know of his celebrity because he made that climb.

A few stories for your consideration of those who started at the bottom:

- Before I became division director at Robert Half International, I was first an entry-level business development associate. Some might define what I did as "grunt work." Every day I pounded the phones for business opportunities, what those "in the biz" called "dialing for dollars." It was the least fun aspect of the job but one that had to be done if you hoped to establish business relationships and build a book of business. My boss taught me as she sat next to me while I made these calls. Each call was followed either by praise for what went right or a lesson on how it could have been better. I went on to start a company and later sold it at six times the earnings before interest, taxes, depreciation, and amortization (EBITDA).
- Andrew Carnegie started as a "bobbin boy," a

person who works in a textile mill and brings bobbins—cylinders or cones holding thread—to the women at the looms. Visions of being a steel tycoon were not dancing in his head yet, but the menial tasks he performed as a bobbin boy laid the groundwork for his success as a baron in the steel industry.

- Ben Franklin, known as the first classic American entrepreneur and businessman, started as an apprentice under his older brother, a printer. Years later he worked for another printer before he founded the *Pennsylvania Gazette*. Franklin first learned the trade, then became his own boss, what some might call the high point of any career.

And one more that is a personal favorite . . .

A young kid from East Harlem had no choice but to start working at an early age to help support his mom. To him this was not unusual. His three older siblings did the same. But once they were married and moved out, the burden fell on him. So, he hustled on the streets to make money wherever he could, even running numbers for bookies, a risky role for a teen.

Eventually, he accepted a job as a messenger at the Bank of Manhattan. One of his responsibilities was to carry boxes of microfiche across town. (Microfiche is a flat piece of film that contained copies of documents, in this case copies of checks or other bank documents.) The bank paid a certain amount for him to catch a cab to get the boxes across town. Instead of taking a taxi, however, he lugged the boxes onto a bus, which was less convenient, so he could pocket the difference between the taxi fee and the bus fare. For a poor kid, every little bit helped.

Two years later, the bank moved him into a training program to become a teller. At the end of each day, he walked across the street to another bank where he worked several over-time hours inputting information into an IBM sorting machine. While the role was basic, it allowed him to make more money to help his mom.

Then he worked in the bookkeeping department of the bank's corporate trust division. Another small step up. As time went by, he accepted a job with Manufacturers Hanover Trust, where he received promotions and became section lead, officer of the bank, and vice president. Over the years, he made his way up the corporate ladder. Eventually, his career segued into life as a consultant as banks began to downsize and restructure.

He never complained about the level of work he did. He always worked hard to increase his knowledge base and increase his usefulness to whomever he worked for. He built an admirable career and an even more admirable life. I know this because he is my dad.

It is unfortunate that the early stage of a person's career is described in negative terms. Phrases like *low man on the totem pole* and words like *gopher*, *peon,* and *grunt* do not paint a pretty picture. They tend to demoralize and make a person feel their labor is unimportant. It takes a mature person to shrug that off, knowing it is not your final station, unless, of course, you choose for it to be so.

But work at this level is important. It is a period of training and education, a time to acquire knowledge that prepares you for what lies ahead. It is the time you define your own point of view, as Bobby Flay learned to do in Jonathan Waxman's kitchen. Working in another man's kitchen helps to sharpen the knives you will use in your own kitchen.

The tireless work of Barack Obama organizing community meetings and running Project Vote, going on the campaign trail, as well as being Chicago's Senator all prepared him for the more difficult role of President of the United States. As Pat Riley sat next to head coach Paul Westhead on the Lakers bench, and next to Chick Hearn at the announcers' table, he developed his own style of coaching. He was not in the top spot but on his way to it. Did Bob Iger have in mind becoming the CEO of the Walt Disney Company when he cleaned gum from a thousand desks? Probably not. But it taught him the value of doing tasks that just need to be done, and it prepared him to be CEO one day.

Look at it like this: the bottom is a place to visit not a place to live.

Why else is starting at the bottom important to your development? What makes that time so significant?

One answer to this question is this: when you start at the bottom, you are subjected to influences—people and experiences—that shape who you are and what type of employee you will become. Something about experiencing that level and knowing what that feels like flavors and seasons your character. As you grind your way to the top, roots go deep that keep you grounded, no matter how lofty the heights you ascend.

There are many influences in winemaking that enhance the wine's flavor. First and foremost, the type of grape. It largely affects the flavor, color, sugar, acidity, and levels of tannin in the wine. But other factors also affect the taste: climate, weather, sunlight, water, warmth (or lack thereof), and nutrients provided by the soil. Different "growing environments" and "conditions" impart flavor components into the wine. Similarly, the environment and condition of life in the cellar, or a period of time at the bottom, will impart various things to you, such as leadership qualities, determination, and a thirst to succeed.

A zillion books have been written about leadership and the traits top leaders possess, and in my opinion, many of those enduring characteristics are developed in the trenches of your initial years in the workforce.

Vince Lombardi, legendary American football coach, considered by many to be the greatest coach in football history, believed leadership habits were not inherited but could be cultivated, like soil. To him, the athletic playing field mirrored the playing field of business. Your work environment is the "field" where traits like tenacity, grit, endurance, discipline, and desire are nurtured.

To avoid toiling in this field is to deprive yourself of the attributes developed there. Tasting what it is like at the bottom does not mean you have to cultivate an appetite for it. But is it essential you know how it tastes.

Jumper Cables

- When it comes to work, everyone has to start somewhere.
- Starting at the bottom teaches you what you need to know to be at the top.
- In winemaking, the "bottom" is working as a cellar assistant, where you clean and sanitize bottling equipment and learn about wine pumps and harvesting equipment. Think about your chosen field. What tasks represent being at the bottom?
- Don't expect to be in the top spot on day one of employment. Be prepared to work your way up.
- Bobby Flay's experience shows a typical career progression. Think of three people you admire and research their careers.
- Think about people you know who have climbed the corporate ladder. What can you learn from their experiences?
- In light of the "bottom" being a period of time for education and training, how would you redefine terms like *low man on the totem pole*, *gofer*, *peon*, and *grunt*?
- Remember: the bottom is a place to visit, not a place to live.

APPENDIX A
THE JUMP-START YOUR CAREER QUICK LIST

At the end of this book on entering the workforce for the first time, I thought it might be useful to collect its concepts in one place. You will find some to be abstract and others more concrete. They represent a source of foundational wisdom—tips to energize the start of your career. It includes lessons I have learned after forty-plus years of employment, if you include my jobs as a kid: paper routes, mowing lawns, shoveling snow, and a window-washing business I called Spot-Free Enterprises. If the engine of your career needs a charge, refer to this list.

Chapter 1

- The best thing you can do for yourself is to identify a career (or calling) that serves as the overarching theme that guides what you do with your time at work.
- Realize that moments of destiny often spring from unexpected events. Oftentimes these occurrences

are propelling you toward what you are meant to do with your life.

- Never underestimate the value of hard work. Even if you possess a sense of destiny, you will have to work your tail off to see it materialize.
- Remember: that which is worth finding is worth working to find.
- Ask yourself, "What will the world fail to see if you do not fulfill your calling?"
- Luck seems to visit the industrious, and it plays a role in their success. Remain diligent, and when luck knocks on your door—and it will—let it in.

Chapter 2

- Mapping out the territory to be explored career-wise is a great first step: time spent making a map sets the stage for your discovery.
- Maps are made to be amended—over time you will need to make adaptations. Accept it. Time is better spent on editing your map than bemoaning the change in your career landscape.
- Using intuition may be an unorthodox ("primitive") way to make sense of your career. That said, it helps redirect your efforts toward making your future a reality. Do not ignore your gut.
- Plans for your career should be big and ambitious. Exceptional enterprises seldom spring from dainty dreams.
- Starting small is never wrong; thinking small is, always.
- The onset of any venture, including your career, is an opportunity at the dream of a lifetime. It is the

perfect time to forsake insignificant objectives, inferior goals, and unimaginative designs.

- Incorporate being mystical—the act of reflection, meditation, and contemplation—into your routine. It increases the potential for big dreams to enter your heart and mind.
- Remember: big dreams become reality by taking little steps.

Chapter 3

- Discoveries may be out of sight, but they are not out of reach.
- You must believe buried treasure exists to dig. Otherwise, why dig?
- Being imaginative is a common trait amongst visionaries who have had success.
- Sometimes work feels monotonous: day-in day-out duties drain us. The best antidote for drudgery is the hope of a discovery.

Chapter 4

- Achievements never happen in a vacuum; others always play a part. Our successes can be traced back to people who assisted us along the way.
- Be liberal in your praise for those who have assisted you.
- There will be occasions we must "go it alone," when you have to stay true to your calling, despite the absence of assistance.

Chapter 5

- Expect to encounter obstacles. You will face a plethora of problems that prevent passage and progress to your discovery. Unobstructed paths to success do not exist; all roads to success are strewn with rubble.
- Consider obstacles—no matter what size they may take—to be confirmation that you are onto something. You are getting closer to your discovery.
- No matter what comes your way, *always* take responsibility for it. Take ownership of your life and your life of employment. Refuse to participate in the blame game, and reject all opportunities to point your finger at people and problems that prevent your progress.
- Remember: taking ownership has a way of turning curses into blessings.

Chapter 6

- Most people assume they have more time than they do and waste more of it than they should. Get busy building your career, but do not rush. Methodically work toward your goal.
- Noteworthy careers develop over time. The care you take in building it is more important that the speed with which you build it.
- There are no overnight successes: successful people toil in anonymity before they achieve acclaim.

Chapter 7

- One of the greatest blessings you have been given is time.
- Do not assume you have more of it than you do. Apply yourself daily to achieve your career goals.
- Do not waste time, but do not rush either. Allow your career to develop.
- "Slow" step-by-step movement toward your career goals should not be confused with inactivity.
- Remember: overnight successes do not exist.
- Let time work its magic. Do not cut corners when it comes to building your career.

Chapter 8

- The career you pursue should reflect your uniqueness: "You have only one thing to offer the world that no one else can give, and that is yourself" (Quentin Crisp).
- The best job is the one that allows you to bring *you* to the job.
- Prize your individuality; avoid being awash in the indistinguishable sameness that characterizes the masses.
- The career you build should be as unique and distinct as you.
- To make your career unlike that of someone else, personalize it.
- Never choose an occupation or job that does not allow you to be your true self.
- Some corporations thrive on uniformity. It is easier to manage staff who are all the same. Other corporations encourage alternate views and

approaches and foster an environment of uniqueness. In my book, those are to be preferred.

- Remember: negative backdrops and challenging environments provide the platform whereby you can stand out in a distinct way.
- Be the best version of yourself, and let your true self make it onto the canvas of your career.

Chapter 9

- As successful as Dr. Weeks was, he never boasted about his accomplishments. He let his work speak for itself.
- Everyone likes to be recognized for a job well done. There will be times your employer misses the opportunity to show you their appreciation.
- The best praise is the kind that is unsolicited. Asking for it diminishes its value.
- Do not be concerned with getting credit for what you have done; be concerned with getting more done.
- Remember: achievements are seldom solo efforts. Thank those who assist you in your career accomplishments.
- If no one else rewards you for a job well done, reward yourself.
- Never forget: no one is indispensable. If a CEO can get fired, so can you.
- If your employer never rewards you for your efforts, it may be time to find an employer who will.

Chapter 10

- When it comes to work, you have to start somewhere. The bottom is as good a place as any.
- When you start at the bottom, you will learn all you need to know to be at the top.
- Careers typically follow a progression from entry-level roles to higher-paying management-related positions.
- The beginning stage of your career, when you feel like the "low man on the totem pole," is a period of training and education, a period that prepares you for bigger roles that come with more responsibility.
- The experience you get from your time at the bottom will help shape the person and leader you will be in the future.

APPENDIX B
RECOMMENDED READING

Bly, Robert. *Iron John: A Book about Men.* Boston: Da Capo Press, 1990.

Bulfinch, Robert. *Bulfinch's Mythology: The Age of Fable, The Age of Chivalry, Legends of Charlemagne.* New York: Random House, Modern Library Edition, 1993.

Campbell, Joseph. *The Hero with a Thousand Faces.* New Jersey: Princeton University Press, 1973.

Cervantes. *Don Quixote.* New York: Vikings Press International Collectors Library, 1951.

Huxley, Aldous. *The Doors of Perception.* New York: First Harper Perennial Modern Classics, 2009.

Huxley, Aldous. *Brave New World.* New York: First Harper Perennial Modern Classics, 2010.

Robert Iger. *The Ride of a Lifetime: Lessons Learned*

from 15 Years as CEO of the Walt Disney Company. New York: Random House, 2019.

Isaacson, Walter. *Steve Jobs.* New York: Simon & Schuster, 2011.

Knight, Phil. *Shoe Dog: A Memoir by the Founder of Nike.* New York: Scribner, 2016.

Krass, Peter, ed. *The Book of Business Wisdom: Classic Writings by the Legends of Commerce and Industry.* New York: John Wiley & Sons, 1997.

Leibovitz, Liel. *Stan Lee: A Life in Comics.* New Haven and London: Yale University Press, 2020.

Lemonick, Michael D. "Egypt: Secrets of the Lost Tomb." *Time*, May 29, 1995, https://content.time.com/time/subscriber/article/0,33009,982362,00.html.

Lombardi, Vince. *Motivation: Lombardi Style.* N.p.: Successories Library, 1992.

McCullough, David. *The Greater Journey: Americans in Paris.* New York: Simon & Schuster, 2011.

Melville, Herman. *Moby Dick; Or, The Whale.* New York: Harper & Brothers, 1851.

Obama, Barack. *A Promised Land.* New York: Crown, 2020.

O'Connor, Ian. *The Captain: The Journey of Derek Jeter.* Boston: Houghton Mifflin Harcourt, 2011.

Parcells, Bill. *Finding A Way to Win: The Principles of Leadership, Teamwork, and Motivation.* New York: Doubleday, 1995.

Pollan, Stephen M., and Mark Levine. *Die Broke: A Radical, Four-Part Financial Plan to Restore Your Confidence, Increase Your Net Worth, and Afford You the Lifestyle of Your Dreams.* New York: HarperBusiness, 1997.

Riley, Pat. *The Winner Within: A Life Plan for Team Players.* New York: Berkley Books, 1993.

Townshend, Pete. *Who I Am: A Memoir.* New York: Harper Perennial, 2012.

SHOUT-OUTS

As I have said, achievements are never solo efforts. That is certainly the case when it comes to this book. Truthfully, it would not have been written without the contributions of a number of amazing people, notwithstanding Michael Klassen with Illumify Media. Throughout the process of writing, he offered constructive ideas on how the material could be shaped to make it more interesting for the reader. When periods of discouragement visited me, he encouraged me to keep at it. I'm at the beginning stages of becoming a writer; the bottom rung comes with some insecurities about what makes it into the page. Mike was a cure for my insecurities. Old friendships rekindled are one of life's better gifts. Mike and his team at Illumify get all the credit for the finished and polished version of this work, including the cover design.

My wife, Stacey, and my daughter, Alex, also need to be thanked. As I have worked to become a better writer, they have tolerated me in all my moods and the highs and lows experienced during the writing process. I knew they loved me, even when they rolled their eyes at me. I am lucky to have a perfect pair of patient supporters who love me for who I am, even when, at times, I am not sure who I am or what I am doing.

To my parents, who mean the world to me. I am fortunate to still have them and to still feel their support in my new endeavors. I have never known a time without their love.

My two college buddies, Dan Amabile and Mark Dane, have prodded me to persist in working on my craft. They have read blurbs, chapters, and stories I have forwarded for their consideration. Despite the material not being up to snuff, never a discouraging word has come from them. Friends who knew you when, another one of life's treasures.

NOTES

Introduction

1. Stephen M. Pollan and Mark Levine, *Die Broke: A Radical, Four-Part Financial Plan to Restore Your Confidence, Increase Your Net Worth, and Afford You the Lifestyle of Your Dreams* (New York: HarperBusiness, 1997), 26.

1. Find Your Calling

1. Pat Riley, *The Winner Within: A Life Plan for Team Players* (New York: Berkley Books, 1993), 62.
2. Barack Obama, *A Promised Land* (New York: Crown, 2020), 69.
3. "Egyptologist Kent Weeks Discusses His Career," The Ancient Egyptian Heritage and Archaeology Fund, YouTube.com video, November 15, 2018, https://www.youtube.com/watch?v=lw5-seKtBR8.

2. Map Out Your Area of Exploration

1. Pete Townshend, *Who I Am: A Memoir* (New York: Harper Perennial, 2012), 4.
2. Peter Krass, ed., *The Book of Business Wisdom: Classic Writings by the Legends of Commerce and Industry* (New York: John Wiley & Sons, 1997), 366–67.
3. Peter Krass, ed., *The Book of Business Wisdom*, 367.

3. Be Ambitious

1. Rona Mann, "Living in the Past – Egyptologist Kent R. Weeks, Old Lyme," InkCT.com, n.d., https://inkct.com/2016/02/kent-weeks/.
2. David McCullough, *The Greater Journey: Americans in Paris* (New York: Simon & Schuster, 2011), 3.
3. Robert Bly, *Iron John: A Book about Men* (Boston: Da Capo Press, 1990), 130.

4. See Unseen Worlds

1. Robert Iger, *The Ride of a Lifetime: Lessons Learned from 15 Years as CEO of the Walt Disney Company* (New York: Random House, 2019), 6.
2. Robert Iger, *The Ride of a Lifetime*, 6.

5. Achievements: The Whole Truth, Nothing but the Truth

1. Steve Johnson, *Where Good Ideas Come From: The Natural History of Innovation* (New York: Riverhead Books, 2010), 35.
2. Joseph Campbell, *The Hero with a Thousand Faces* (Princeton, NJ: Princeton University Press, 1973), 22.

6. Doors First, Then Discoveries: Expect Obstacles

1. Michael D. Lemonick, "Egypt: Secrets of the Lost Tomb," *Time*, May 29, 1995, https://content.time.com/time/subscriber/article/0,33009,982362,00.html.

7. The Importance of Time

1. Anna Russell, "How Bernardine Evaristo Conquered British Literature," *The New Yorker*, NewYorker.com, February 3, 2022, https://www.newyorker.com/culture/persons-of-interest/how-bernardine-evaristo-conquered-british-literature.

8. The Uniqueness of You

1. Aldous Huxley, *Brave New World Revisited and Brave New World Revisited* (New York: HarperPerennial, 2004), 256.
2. Liel Leibovitz, *Stan Lee: A Life in Comics* (New Haven and London: Yale University Press, 2020), 5.

9. Let Your Work Speak for Itself

1. Bill Parcells, *Finding a Way to Win: The Principles of Leadership, Teamwork, and Motivation* (New York: Doubleday, 1995), 188.
2. Saxon White Kessinger, "Indispensable Man," 1959, https://appleseeds.org/indispen-man_saxon.htm.

10. The Bottom Is as Good a Place as Any to Start

1. Bobby Flay, *Bobby Flay's Mesa Grill Cookbook: Explosive Flavors from the Southwestern Kitchen* (New York; Clarkson Potter/Publishers, 2007), 1.

2. Bobby Flay, *Bobby Flay's Mesa Grill Cookbook*, 1.

ABOUT THE AUTHOR

Chris Fontanella is the founder of Encore Professionals Group, a professional services firm specializing in the identification and placement of accounting and finance candidates in temporary and permanent positions. He previously served as Division Director for Robert Half International and Client Service Director for Resources Global Professionals.

Prior to entering the staffing industry, he spent years studying theology and preparing for ministry, having received his bachelor's degree from Oral Roberts University and his master's from Fuller Theological Seminary. Chris is also the author of *Against the Grain: Counterintuitive Ideas on Business and Life*, a unique account of the atypical philosophies behind his own success in the competitive staffing industry.

Chris continues to provide staffing services through Encore while he explores the world of writing and publication.

CPSIA information can be obtained
at www.ICGtesting.com
Printed in the USA
BVHW071020171222
654331BV00013B/994